Randolph Caldecott
An Illustrated Life

Claudette Hegel

Avisson Press Inc.
Greensboro

First Edition
Printed in the United States of America

Library of Congress Cataloging-in-Publication Data

Hegel, Claudette.
    Randolph Caldecott; an illustrated life/Claudette Hegel.—1st ed.
    p.cm.— (Avisson young adult series)
    Summary: A biography of the nineteenth-century English artist
    and illustrator whose sixteen picture books "greatly influenced
    children's book illustration" and, for whom the Caldecott Medal
    is named.
    Includes bibliographical references and index.
    ISBN 1-888105-60-7 (lib. bndg.)
        1-888105-68-2 (tr. paper)
    1. Caldecott, Randolph, 1846-1886—Juvenile literature. 2.
    Illustrators—England—Biography—Juvenile literature.
    [1. Caldecott, Randolph, 1846-1886. 2. Illustrators.] 1. Title.
    II. Series.
    NC978.5.C3H44 2004
    741.6'42'092—dc22
    [B]
                                                    2003057771

Bookplate of Mr. Seaman (p.123) and frontispiece photo, courtesy of Houghton Library, Cambridge, MA. The "Statuette of a Cat" (p.51), courtesy of The Victoria and Albert Museum, London, England. The Horn Book cover by Maurice Sendak (p.114), reprinted   by permission of The Horn Book Inc., Boston, MA.

3918

Acknowledgments

The author wishes to extend grateful appreciation to the following people for their invaluable assistance in completing this book: Keeling Anthony of the Randolph Caldecott Society—UK; Martin Durrant of the Victoria and Albert Museum; Lauren Raece of *The Horn Book Magazine*; Jennie Rathbun of the Houghton Library of Harvard University; Gwen Reichert of the Randolph Caldecott Society of America.

Dedication

This book is dedicated to the members of the
Randolph Caldecott Society UK and the Randolph
Caldecott Society of America. They are kindred
spirits in my appreciation of Caldecott and his work.

Contents

List of Illustrations

Introduction

Who Was Randolph Caldecott?

MOST PEOPLE INTERESTED in children's books have noticed a Caldecott Medal sticker on some picture books. The American Library Association awards the annual prize to a picture book illustrator. The sticker represents the book considered the "most distinguished American picture book for children's literature" of the previous year.

Who was Randolph Caldecott, the one for whom the award is named? Caldecott, a nineteenth-century artist and illustrator, is known primarily for the sixteen picture books he illustrated in the 1870s and 1880s. Although he spent only about 14 years as a professional artist, Caldecott greatly influenced children's book illustration.

Maurice Sendak, Caldecott Medalist for *Where the Wild Things Are*, said, "Caldecott's work heralds the beginning of the modern picture book . . . Words are left out—but the picture says it. Pictures are left out—but the word says it." He compares Caldecott's illustrations to music, not just because the characters are often singing, dancing, or playing instruments, but because they often appear ready for music. Sendak called his 1965 book *Hecter Protector and As I Went over the Water* "an intentionally contrived homage to this beloved teacher." The two Mother Goose rhymes in the book become more developed and detailed through the illustrations in the manner Caldecott illustrated not only his Picture Books, but also his illustrations for other books and magazines.

Randolph Caldecott changed the way picture books are illustrated. Before Caldecott, illustrations simply reflected a story or poem exactly as the words described. Caldecott's illustrations added to the story. For example, in one illustration in *Bye, Baby Bunting* Caldecott showed the baby clothed in a rabbit skin. The baby seems to be figuring out that the new rabbit coat used to be a live bunny like the ones on the hillside.

Author Hilda van Stockum thought his illustrations so lively she said, "Caldecott provided me with my first movies" and "even the grass on the ground adds to the general effect."

Caldecott eagerly studied art whenever possible, although he was largely self-taught; he attended two art schools only briefly. He rarely left his home without a notebook handy to sketch whatever appealed to him. He spent many school hours engaged in drawing. Even after he began working in a bank, he often sketched on the bank forms he completed. His personal letters usually contained at least one sketch. He also practiced various art mediums continually, both before and after he made art his career.

Caldecott's optimism and zest for his art may have helped prolong his life. He rarely let the chronic illness from his childhood bout with rheumatic fever interfere with his work or his general character. Writer, editor, and friend Henry Blackburn said he'd never heard a word spoken against Caldecott and called him "a man of whom all spoke well."

Another friend wrote, "Caldecott's ability was general, not special. It found its natural and most agreeable outlet in art and humour, but everybody who knew him, and those who received his letters, saw that there were perhaps a dozen ways in which he would have distinguished himself had he been drawn to them."

Although Caldecott died in 1886, a month short of his 40th birthday, his influence still lives. One of his friends said Caldecott's name would "remain till the end of our art and literature a household word."

As Hilda van Stockum said, "So let us take off our hats to that deftest of all gentlemen, that humorist, that artist, that friend—Randolph Caldecott."

Chapter One

Childhood

THE WALLED CITY of Chester in Cheshire, England, had its beginnings in 1330. The early citizens built the city on old Roman ruins next to the River Dee.

Centuries later, people built continuous covered porches along their homes on Bridge Street. The porches, called walks, were located on the outsides of the buildings between the first and second stories. Many stairways led to the street below. People called Bridge Street "The Rows" from the appearance of the walks lining the street.

John Caldecott and Mary Dinah Brookes Caldecott, who married on September 27, 1842, lived at 150 Bridge Street (now #16) halfway down The Rows.

The Caldecott coat of arms is based on the Heraldic description: "Arms: Argent, a fess Azure fretted Or between three Cinquefoils Gules. Crest: On a wreath an Ostrich proper." The coat of arms motto is *In Utrumque Paratus*, which means "In either situation ready." The Caldecotts had to be ready for the changes to their family over the next few years.

The Caldecotts' first son, John, was born on June 23, 1843. The following year another son, William, was born on August 31. The Caldecott family didn't increase in 1845, but on March 22, 1846, another son was born. Mr. and Mrs. Caldecott named their new son Randolph.

Tragedy struck in late August of that year. Young William died as the result of convulsions four days short of his second birthday. Randolph was only five months old at the time and didn't have a chance to get to know his older brother.

The remaining brothers, John and Randolph, gained a younger sister named Sophia on June 2, 1848. The family moved to Challoner House on Crook Street that same year.

Another girl named Elizabeth was born on November 30, 1849. Baby Elizabeth died just six weeks and two days later.

On November 9, 1850, The Caldecott family increased again with the birth of Alfred. Another boy named Harold was born on April 14, 1852.

The Caldecott family lived above a shop where John Caldecott worked as a woolen draper, tailor, and hatter. Little natural light came through the tiny windows of the shop. The hot, steamy shop always smelled strongly of wet wool. Randolph and Alfred shared a small, stuffy room above the shop. The boys must have enjoyed the fresh country air during their occasional extended visits with relatives on a farm near Malpas.

In August 1852, when Randolph was only six years old, both he and his mother became ill with rheumatic fever. On August 21, Mary died of the illness in a house on Hamilton Street in Hoole. The only likeness Randolph ever had of his mother was a drawing he made from memory.

Randolph's father married Maria Guest on December 12, 1854. John and Maria Caldecott had at least six more children. That meant Randolph had six brothers and sisters, two who died very young, and at least six more half-brothers and half-sisters.

That many children must have made the family's home life quite active, but Randolph often had to miss the more active playtimes. He survived the bout of rheumatic fever, but his brother Alfred later said the illness left Randolph "always delicate." Randolph Caldecott made references to his illness throughout his life, but rarely complained. Instead, he often poked fun at his limitations. He accepted the illness and learned to adjust his lifestyle to accommodate his condition.

Randolph's condition caused him to tire easily. He couldn't take part in many physical activities like other children. Luckily, Randolph always enjoyed drawing, reading, carving in wood, and molding with clay. His favorite subject in his artwork was animals. He happily sat with his books or art materials while other children played active games.

Randolph didn't always sit still. He preferred to spend his time wandering around the countryside rather than studying. Even so, his teacher appointed Randolph "head boy" (the student assistant to the headmaster). The teacher, Mr. Harris, called Randolph and Alfred Caldecott "two of the best boys in school." Mr. Harris also said Randolph had "an infinite faculty for taking pains."

At least Randolph and Alfred among the Caldecott brothers attended school at Henry VII School (or Henry VIII School, according to some sources), also known as

King's School. At the time, the school was attached to the Chester Cathedral. John Caldecott let his sons continue their studies long after most boys their ages were learning a trade.

Arthur Locker, who wrote the preface to *The Complete Collection of Randolph Caldecott's Contributions to the "Graphic"*, found one of Randolph's old schoolbooks at a bookstall. Locker said Randolph's drawings in the book showed "no more special talent than is shown by scores of lads who have a turn for drawing."

Randolph admired the carved scenes pictured on the dean's and vice dean's stalls at school. These carvings showed pilgrims praying for the powers of healing at the Shrine of St. Werburgh.

Since 1541, school classes were held in the refectory, the room monks once used as a dining room. The classroom with a total of about 20 students was Randolph's favorite room in the cathedral. Carved beams crisscrossed the refectory walls. A pulpit with decorative carvings stood on a raised dais. In earlier times, monks on this platform read to the other monks during meals.

Randolph once painted a watercolor picture of the refectory the way he thought it looked in the times of the monks. He used shades of brown for nearly everything in the picture: the monks' robes, the rough planks used as tables, the carved beams, and the walls.

He looked at his work and decided the scene looked too drab and uninteresting. Randolph added a gleam in the eye of one monk and a squirrel hiding among the rafters. Suddenly the painting gained a life of its own.

Mr. Harris saw the painting, but didn't say anything

at first. Randolph feared his teacher disapproved of his adding a little humor to the painting. After all, monks lived lives of total religious sacrifice.

The day after Mr. Harris saw the painting, Randolph discovered his painting framed and hanging on the back wall of the school. The painting remained there for many years.

Mr. Harris knew Randolph had talent. The teacher suggested Randolph attend the Chester School of Art. Randolph told him his father didn't think drawing was real work for a man and actually discouraged his artistic tendencies. John Caldecott thought only people with lots of money and nothing better to do should spend time on art.

Mr. Harris visited John Caldecott to discuss the possibility of sending Randolph for art instruction. Mr. Caldecott agreed to let Randolph attend the Chester School of Art every Saturday morning. Within a year Randolph had learned all he could from the teacher, but continued to practice his art whenever he could.

To pay for the lessons at the art school, Randolph agreed to work in his father's shop after school each day and all day during summer vacation. John Caldecott hoped Randolph would learn to enjoy working in the shop, despite the air quality of the shop worsening his state of health.

The elder Caldecott didn't get his wish. Randolph never learned to enjoy the work and had no interest in taking over the shop. Alfred entered the service of the Church when he finished school and became known for his musical compositions. He also wrote a version of

"Aesop's Fables," which Randolph illustrated

John Caldecott was disappointed that none of his other children showed an interest in the family business either. The family moved to 23 Richmond Place at Boughton just outside Chester in 1860. Randolph's father then became an accountant.

John Caldecott must have seen merit in working with numbers. He encouraged Randolph to become a banker. Randolph approved of the idea. In 1861, the year after the family moved to Boughton, Randolph traded his school studies for work as a bank clerk. He had attended school about five years longer than most children at the time. Many children started working in the local mills by the age of ten. Randolph Caldecott's childhood officially ended when he was 15 years old.

Chapter Two
Early Working Life

AT ONE TIME, Randolph Caldecott's father lived in Whitchurch, a town about 20 miles south of Chester. John Caldecott arranged for his son to work as a clerk for the Whitchurch and Ellesmere Bank in Whitchurch.

Caldecott approved of his father's decision. His weak lungs and heart forced him to find work that wasn't strenuous. He thought the air would be healthier in a bank than in the family hat shop. In 1861, at the age of fifteen, Caldecott moved to Whitchurch. Until that time, he'd never been more than a few miles from Chester.

Caldecott moved in with a young married couple named William and Charlotte Brown. They lived in an old farmhouse near Wirswall, about two miles from Whitchurch. Caldecott enjoyed the area because, in addition to hunting and fishing, he was able to attend many county fairs and cattle markets. These events provided many scenes for him to sketch.

Most of the time, Caldecott walked to and from work. He often arrived for work at the bank or home for supper just in time or even a little late. He had a tendency to stop to make an entry or two in the sketchbook he always carried.

Caldecott's sketch of his banking days in Manchester.

In time, Caldecott sketched most of what he saw on his travels between the farm and the bank. A variety of animals, buildings, fences, trees, a stile, and more were carefully recorded in his sketchbooks. Many of these sketches became the basis for future illustrations.

Whitchurch was the market center, particularly for the dairy industry, for many of the surrounding areas. As part of his job, Caldecott visited other small villages. He enjoyed this task. He not only made many friends, but also found many things to sketch.

At one point, Caldecott tried to make some extra money selling life insurance. Friend James M. Etches told about one of Caldecott's experiences with the second job. A "wary farmer" agreed to buy £500 worth of life insurance and completed the necessary forms. At the time the farmer made his first payment, he wanted to make sure he understood the policy. The farmer thought that if he were still alive in a year he'd be paid the £500. After Caldecott explained that the money would be paid to the man's family only if the farmer died, the farmer put his money in his pocket and walked out. That's the closest Caldecott ever came to selling an insurance policy.

Caldecott learned to be satisfied with the pay and duties of his job at the bank. Luckily he enjoyed working on the math associated with his job as well as talking with customers. Most of the work at the bank was copying or adding long columns of numbers. The sketching helped relieve the boredom of the work for Caldecott and his fellow employees.

Caldecott sketched whenever he had a few moments. He drew on deposit slips, envelopes, desk blotters, note paper, and any other scrap of paper he could find. Subjects were often bank customers or fellow employees, as well as animals, particularly horses and dogs.

Many of the sketches contained elements of humor. Caldecott became known for his lively nature and practical jokes. In an August 18, 1885, letter to friend and fellow bank clerk William Clough, Caldecott said, "As for me, I am sure I must have caused him [Walter Smith, another bank employee] moments of dissatisfaction and uneasiness. There was seldom in me any steady sober respect for the work of a bank." Letters and drawings Caldecott sent to Clough were sold at Sotheby's auction house in 1925, 20 years after Clough's death.

Even if Caldecott thought he may not have been the

best worker at the bank, the records his employers kept about their employees' work show that Caldecott "did it well."

One of Caldecott's managers asked to see him one day. The manager complimented Caldecott's work, but asked him to stop sketching on deposit slips and other bank paper. The manager also asked Caldecott to change his desk blotter since sketches of animals chasing each other was "not proper" for a bank.

The manager may not have wanted his employee to sketch on bank forms, but he appreciated Caldecott's talent. The manager took a sketch of himself on bank stationery home for his wife.

Caldecott's first drawing was published while working at the Whitchurch and Ellesmere Bank. His illustration of the fire at the Queen Railway Hotel (now called the Queen's Hotel) appeared in the December 7, 1861, issue of the *Illustrated London News*. Customers visited the bank just to see the artist who had a drawing published. People treated him like a celebrity when he visited Chester for Christmas. Even Caldecott's father, who didn't completely approve of his son's artistic pursuits, was impressed when the illustration appeared in print.

Caldecott largely enjoyed his work and had many friends in Whitchurch. In a January 17, 1875, letter to a friend in Manchester, he said, "I often think of the scenes and faces and jokes of banking days, and have amongst them many pleasant reminiscences."

The primary problem Caldecott had living in Whitchurch concerned the lack of other artists in the area. He felt a need to belong to an artist group where he could discuss his work.

On December 24, 1866, Caldecott met William Langton, the managing director of the Manchester and Salford Bank in Manchester. Langton hired Caldecott to be a clerk in his bank, which later became known as Williams and Glyn's Bank.

Caldecott packed his belongings for the move to Manchester. Mrs. Brown asked him for a sketch or two to hang on the wall. He gave her three. One sketch showed the farm, another the family, and one the surrounding area.

The work at the Manchester and Salford Bank demanded more concentration than the job at the Whitchurch bank. In a January 17, 1870, letter to Matthew Noble, a fellow clerk, Caldecott said, "The sweet bonds of friendship between clerks are now and then temporarily broken asunder by the bad-tempered engendered of a round of dreary, shut-up, daily drudgery. The noble soul will, however, soar above such petty work and meandering among the ever-recurring sentiments of a thoughtful mind will find sufficient intellectual food upon which to fatten and grow fat."

Sometimes Caldecott didn't enjoy the required duties as an employee of a bank. In a September 27, 1868, letter to friend John Lennox, he said, "I, who am not naturally formed for work. . . . A thought occurs to me here—what the deuce are we all working and sweating for? Why give ourselves so much unnecessary trouble about 'little things'? What more do we require besides health, food and clothing?"

Caldecott did enjoy going to customer homes on bank business because he missed living in the country. He took long walks out of the city whenever possible, and visiting customers allowed him to walk during work hours. While walking, he could often stop to do a sketch or two.

During his time in Manchester, Caldecott lived on Aberdeen Street, Rusholme Grove, and Bowden. Living in Manchester proved to be helpful to Caldecott as an artist. He joined the Brasenose Club, an organization devoted to artists. He met many fellow artists, some of whom also became friends.

The people of Manchester appreciated art. The area inspired Caldecott and allowed him to learn more about art. Many times, he worked at the bank all day, then spent the entire night working on his art.

James Blower, another bank clerk, once saw Caldecott do a sketch during a lunch break. Blower said Caldecott should have his work exhibited. The next month, several of Caldecott's paintings and sketches of city and country life were included at a Brasenose Exhibition at the Royal Manchester Institution.

In the spring of 1870, Caldecott took some of his sketches to London. Many editors recognized Caldecott's talent. One editor offered him a job illustrating at *Pictorial World*. The job would have paid Caldecott over £500 a year, about five times what the bank paid him. A friend advised Caldecott to turn down the offer since he thought Caldecott's art had the potential to produce much more income than that.

In early 1872, Caldecott sold a small oil painting and

a watercolor painting, which gave him the courage to quit his job at the bank and move to London to try to make a living from his art. He said, "I had the money in my pocket sufficient to keep me for a year of so, and was hopeful that during that time my powers would be developed and my style improved so much that I should find plenty of work."

Even if he couldn't find work right away, Caldecott prepared himself to go hungry if it meant he could work on his art full time. Although he was able to make a living from his art and never had to work in a bank again, he appreciated the training the bank work had given him. The experience working with numbers at the bank helped him manage both his personal finances and his business as an illustrator.

Chapter Three

Personal Life

RANDOLPH CALDECOTT USUALLY wished to have his personal life kept private. He preferred to be known for his work. Even so, many of his letters to friends and even business associates contained personal information.

A few photographs were taken of Caldecott, but no known photograph or illustration of him without his beard is known to exist, as beards were the style during his lifetime.

Marian Caldecott, who likely knew her husband better than anyone else, commented on the photograph of Caldecott engraved by Henry Watkinson by saying, "It is the one I think the best, but some people do not like it because the expression is too grave, they consider, and he looks ill. It is, however, exactly like my husband."

She also said of the last photograph taken of Caldecott, "His friends think that he looks sad and ill, but I feel that this is more like him than any of the others."

Walter Crane, a well-known artist, described Caldecott as tall and handsome with light brown hair and gray-blue eyes. He further described Caldecott as a man who "never looked strong, and his quiet manner, low voice and gentle but rather serious and earnest way of speaking did not suggest extraordinary vivacity and humour of his drawings, though an occasional humorous remark may have betrayed a glimpse of such qualities."

A bank coworker described Caldecott by saying, "The handsome lad carried his own recommendation. With light brown hair falling with a ripple over his brow, blue-grey eyes shaded by long lashes, sweet and mobile mouth, tall and well-made, he joined to these physical advantages a gay good humour and a charming disposition. No wonder then that he was a general favourite."

After Caldecott's death, William Clough, a friend and coworker at the Manchester and Salford Bank, described Caldecott's character and personality by saying, "If the art, tender and true as it is, be not of the highest, yet the artist is expressed in his work as perhaps few others have been. Nothing to be regretted—all of the clearest—an open-air, pure life—a clean soul. Wholesome as the England he loved so well. Manly, tolerant, and patient under suffering. None of the friends he made did he let go. No envy, malice, or uncharitableness spoiled him; no social flattery or fashionable success, made him forget those he had known in the early years."

In 1873, Caldecott looked at himself with a touch of humor. He described himself at the time by saying, "My life is a precious one, the eyes of the world are upon me, and I have lost somewhat of that much admired, greatly envied, free, gay, dashing, devil-may-care, adventurous, heroic, and reckless spirit which lent to my youth an excitement and a charm (here I turn away and drop a tear—

a manly tear—for as the years go by I change. I am not as I was).''

In a July 18, 1882, letter enclosed with a photograph to Walter Wilson of the Institute of Painters in Water Colour, Caldecott described himself in the P.S. as "Pale complexion, hair light, beard fair, height 5' 11 in." The "pale complexion" Caldecott spoke about may have been from physical ailments. His childhood bout with rheumatic fever left him with a weak heart. Toward the end of his life, he also suffered from tuberculosis (called "consumption" in Caldecott's time) and stomach problems.

Caldecott seldom mentioned his health problems. If he did say something about his health, he usually approached the subject with humor. In a letter to his friend from Whitchurch William Etches dated March 28, 1873, he said he "Had several smart attacks on the heart, a little wounded once, causing that machine to go up and down like a lamb's tail when its owner is partaking of the nourishment provided by bounteous Nature." About a month later, Caldecott wrote, "I only danced twenty-one times at the last ball." In his Picture Book *The Babes in the Wood*, he drew himself as the sick father sticking out his tongue for the doctor.

Living in the polluted atmosphere of Manchester made Caldecott's health worse. Dust always hung in the air from the coal-burning textile mills in the area. He escaped the polluted air of the city for the country whenever possible. His health was another reason besides wanting to earn his living as an artist that he moved to London in 1872.

SORE SICKE THEY WERE
AND LIKE TO DYE

Caldecott faced many health problems in his lifetime, a fact
that he incorporated into his sketches, as in this illustration
from *The Babes in the Wood*.

In the fall of 1876, William Clough asked Caldecott
to visit him. Caldecott replied in an October 6 letter, "I
am only just recovering from a little illness which might
have developed into a great illness and I do not like to go
out much—the weather of this morning not being prom-
ising—otherwise I should go down to the Bank."

Later that month, Caldecott's doctor advised him to

move to a healthier climate. Caldecott first went to Buxton in Derbyshire for a few weeks, then to the Riviera and northern Italy near Christmas. At the time, Caldecott couldn't climb two flights of stairs without stopping to rest. Even so, he always replied, "Quite well, thank you," when someone asked about his health.

In late 1878, Caldecott was in the southern part of France. He said, "I have come here in order that rheumatism may forget me and not recognise me on return to Albion's shores."

The climate must have done him well. In a letter to friend Frederick Locker-Lampson, for whom he also did some illustrating, dated February 26, 1879, Caldecott wrote, "Had all my friends who think I am delicate seen me capering about they would have rejoyced at the apparent recovery of youthful energy and mirth."

Caldecott's health may have been better if he had taken better care of himself. He smoked cigarettes and a pipe. At one point, he also drank alcohol more than he would have liked. In a March 28, 1879, letter, he answered William Clough's caution to be careful not to get consumption by saying, "Consumption be damned! It's consumption of cigarettes and Chianti—capri and Falernian. I have as fine an appetite as a man could wish and as strong a drinketite as in the glorious 'Crown' days (nearly)." He went on to say that eating in hotel restaurants for a few months gave him a "chronic dyspepsia."

Caldecott's good humor showed through in many of his letters. Comical sketches, often poking fun at himself, appeared on much of Caldecott's correspondence. Other sketches were more serious. Often sketches enclosed the address of where he was living or visiting. In one sketch a man points to the address and in another several women are reading a sign with Caldecott's address. The letters he wrote while staying in the country included many sketches of outdoor scenes. His letters from London or other cities had fewer sketches and fewer outdoor scenes.

Caldecott lived in several places in his life. He spent the first fifteen years of his life in Chester. He then moved to Whitchurch to begin his banking career. After he realized Whitchurch couldn't fulfill his artistic needs, he moved to Manchester. He finally ended his banking career when, in 1872, he moved to London to pursue his art full time.

In London, Caldecott lived and worked at 46 Great Russell Street the first six years of his art career. He didn't have to go far to do some types of research since his home was near the British Museum.

On July 21, 1872, Caldecott wrote a letter to a friend in Manchester and said, "London is of course the proper place for a young man for seeing the manners and customs of society, and for getting a living in some of the less frequented grooves of human labour, but for a residence give me a rural or marine retreat. I sigh for some 'cool sequestered spot,' the world forgetting, by the world forgot." The accompanying sketch titled "A cool sequestered spot" shows Caldecott sitting in a tub with a plate of food in one hand and a bottle of liquor in the other.

Even though he spent much of his time pursuing his art, Caldecott was often lonely the first few years he lived in London. Of the people with which he wanted to associate, Caldecott said, "I prefer a free-drinker and a union-of-souls-sort-of-chap to a miser or a cold-blooded cove." Many of Caldecott's friends included business associates, but only certain ones.

William Slagg thought Caldecott would benefit by meeting Thomas Armstrong, an artist who became the art director of the South Kensington Museum. Slagg was the brother of a portrait painter, both of whom may have been Caldecott's associates at the Brasenose Club. Slagg gave Caldecott a letter of introduction to meet Armstrong. The two artists immediately liked one another. Armstrong not only served as Caldecott's artistic advisor and collaborator in interior design, but also became Caldecott's closest friend. In a November 2, 1876, letter to Henry Blackburn, Caldecott wrote, "Pen can never put down how much I owe, in many ways, to T.S. [Thomas Armstrong]."

Armstrong, who was fourteen years older than Caldecott, became almost like an older brother to Caldecott. The two met almost daily while Caldecott lived in London. They spent most holidays together.

Caldecott spent January 1877 at the Hotel Splendid in Menton on the French Riviera. Thomas Armstrong was also staying at the hotel at the time. The two friends spent much of their time painting and sketching the area. Going to other areas to "rest" was not possible for Caldecott because he was always in pursuit of his art and did little resting. Luckily, simply a change in climate often proved to be beneficial for his health.

By the time Caldecott returned to London, people's

interest in books had increased greatly. Book stalls appeared everywhere, even in railway stations. The increase in reading corresponded with an increase in Caldecott's work. Even while in Italy and on the Riviera, Caldecott sent letters and sketches to his contacts in London.

As Caldecott got more work, the more famous he became. People wanted to know more about his personal life. Many people thought Caldecott and Kate Greenaway, another foremost illustrator for children, were married. Caldecott and Greenaway, sometimes called the "twin illustrators" because Greenaway was only five days older than Caldecott, were friends and exchanged letters and visits.

When William Clough mentioned a possible romance between the twin illustrators, Caldecott replied in his November 8, 1879, letter, "She is, as you ask me, nearly thirty—maybe more—and not beautiful." She should have been flattered, even with the "not beautiful" comment, because she was 33 years old at the time, the same age as Caldecott himself.

Caldecott wasn't married at the time, but spent much of his time with friends. Henry Blackburn, one of Caldecott's editors, had a reputation of being difficult for artists to please and could sometimes be mean-spirited. Even so, he and Caldecott became friends as well as business associates. Blackburn said of Caldecott, "He would do anything in an emergency to aid a friend—or a foe, if he had known one—but neither health nor inclination led him in that direction."

During the summers of 1872, 1873, and 1874, Caldecott often stayed at a cottage Blackburn owned. The cottage, on an estate named Farnham Royal, was located three miles north of Slough in Buckinghamshire near Windsor. Blackburn said the location was "the picturesque neighbourhood of Stoke Pogis and Burnham Beeches." The cottage at Farnham Royal was demolished to make way for a new road in 1958.

While at Farnham Royal, Caldecott used "a loose box adjoining a stable" as his studio. Normally used as a place for a horse to move around more freely than in a stall, the loose box contained all the supplies he needed in addition to a table and chairs. He even had an American hammock in one corner where he could rest. One of the projects he worked on at Farnham Royal was *Old Christmas: From the Sketch Book of Washington Irving.*

After a few years Caldecott decided he needed a country home, partially on his doctor's recommendation. He remembered the life at Farnham Royal. He thought living in the country would slow his pace and therefore help his health.

In 1879, Caldecott either bought or rented a home called Wybournes, located at Kemsing, a small village near Sevenoaks in Kent. He described the location of his home as "an out-of-the-way place, but exactly right for me." The small house had an old-fashioned garden and many tame animals in residence, as well as many wild animal visitors.

Caldecott described the inside of his new home in a letter to William Clough on November 8, 1879. He said, "I have no curtains and no carpet in this room; but I have 2 Scinde rugs on the floor; I have borrowed the drawing-

A sketch of Caldecott's home, Wybournes, near Sevenoaks.

room fender (its only piece of furniture) and a few things from the dining-parlour, and I am warm and cosy. My bedroom just holds a bed and an adjoining room holds the other things."

He lived at Wybournes alone at first. Several years earlier in a November 3, 1873, letter to William Etches, Caldecott said, "Ah, well, as each of my young friends gets married I feel older and sadder and yet see more for me to toil and struggle for. Though I get somewhat stouter without, yet I feel a little hollower within, and as nature abhors a vacuum, let's open a bottle and take a deep, deep, &c."

Nearly six years later in an April 3, 1879, letter to Etches, Caldecott said, "I am getting an old fogy now, Will! People put their daughters and nieces under my charge for walks in romantic valleys or for prowls on promenades to view fireworks."

Thoughts of marriage were on Caldecott's mind. He

met a young woman named Marian Brind, who lived with her family near Chelsfield. Her father, Frederick Brind, was a wine merchant and served as a Church warden.

How Caldecott and Marian met is unknown, but Caldecott soon announced his engagement to her. Horatia Gatty, the editor of *Aunt Judy's Magazine*, sent her congratulations on his upcoming marriage and also asked him several questions. Caldecott replied, "I have not time this morning to give you any of the particulars for which you yearn—except the name—which is at present—Marian Harriet Brind—she resides about 7 miles from here (nothing to a good horse)."

In a March 11, 1880, letter to William Clough, Caldecott said, "You say, bold flatterer, that *she* must be very good to deserve me. Her friends say that I am a lucky man and am to be unaffectedly congratulated—so I think. Therefore all ought to be well and future happiness secured."

In the same letter to Clough, Caldecott included a sketch of three men sitting on a rail fence. He described the scene as "The 3 are waiting until what they consider to be the proper moment for entering the adjacent church and taking up their stand at the Hymeneal altar. . . . It is a sketch of a probable scene on the 18th morning of this month—if fine weather. For your ancient companion of the ledger and the scales of brass purposes to drive in a dog-cart—most rustically—with his best man and his curati (for to assist one Alfred Caldecott [Randolph's brother], of Christchurch, Stafford) to some decent and comfortable railing near the Church at which he has in-

Caldecott married Marian Brind in 1880. He enjoyed having a life companion, as seen in this happy sketch of a couple being looked upon by lovebirds.

vited his wife-elect to meet him on the aforesaid morn." Caldecott goes on to talk of his nervousness and thoughts of the future and past days of bachelorhood. He said "ever and anon he will ask himself if he really put the ring in his pocket."

On March 18, 1880, Marian walked from her home next to the church of St. Martin-of-Tours in Chelsfield. F. B. Seaman, a banker who served as best man, drove the groom to the wedding in a dog-cart. On the way, Caldecott sold his mare to Seaman. After his marriage, Caldecott gave up his gig and started using a horse and buggy for transportation.

One of the responsibilities Frederick Brind had in 1880 was overseeing having the bells of the church rehung. It's possible the bells were not hanging in the church at the time of the wedding and could not be rung to announce the marriage.

The Chelsfield church where Randolph and Marian Caldecott were married was heavily damaged during World War II, but was restored in 1950.

Some of the happiest times in Caldecott's life were after his marriage. Although Marian was very important to him, Caldecott doesn't specifically mention her very often in his letters. After his marriage the "I" in his letters often became "we."

Caldecott and his wife went nearly everywhere together from the time they were married. After a honeymoon in Menton (or, as one source stated, a honeymoon in Venice), Marian moved in with Randolph at Wybournes. Even though Caldecott enjoyed his wife's company, he kept regular working hours. He said he would have "Breakfast at eight—and no nonsense. Work from nine to two."

Caldecott's time at Wybournes was one of the happiest, healthiest, and most productive times of his life. Even so, the Caldecotts left Wybournes and moved to London in 1882. Their tall, narrow-fronted Georgian house was located at 24 Holland Street, a small, quiet street near the South Kensington Museum (now the Victoria and Albert Museum). Wybournes burned down about 1900.

The Caldecotts missed the country. Before a year passed, they took a 21-year lease on Broomfield, a country house in Frensham, Farnham, Surrey. The home at Holland Street became a studio for Caldecott.

Broomfield was so dirty when the Caldecotts took

over, they couldn't put their things inside until the place was cleaned. The Caldecotts soon discovered neither the house nor the climate was to their liking. They both missed Wybournes. They lived in Frensham only three years, then returned to live in the house on Holland Street in London.

After he decided to leave Broomfield, Caldecott wrote a letter to Frederick Locker-Lampson dated July 10, 1885. He said, "There are many objects, views, bits of building in landscape, besides beasts and birds, which I have been so handy to my sketchbook that I have neglected them."

Caldecott's love of art obviously spilled over into his personal life. His personal life, particularly his chronic illness, sometimes interfered with his art. Caldecott spent most of his 40 years getting the greatest enjoyment he could out of both his personal and business lives

Chapter Four

Hobbies and Interests

MOST OF RANDOLPH CALDECOTT'S life centered around art. The childhood illness that caused him to tire easily throughout his life may have helped him focus on his art from an early age. His artistic pursuits were not as strenuous as other activities.

Caldecott's condition made physical activity difficult. That didn't stop him from continually exploring the countryside or the city by walking, riding a horse, or riding in a carriage. He enjoyed hunting, fishing, and attending markets and cattle fairs. If his sketches are any indication, he may have enjoyed ice skating and lawn tennis, at least to watch even if his health wouldn't permit him to participate.

Activities with horses were some of Caldecott's favorite pastimes. He enjoyed riding horses and riding in a gig, a two-wheeled carriage pulled by a horse. Business associate and friend Henry Blackburn said that once in 1878 Caldecott was disappointed when he and Blackburn "had to take a trap instead with a driver." Caldecott had wanted to drive the horse himself. Of course, if someone else drove the horse or horses, Caldecott could work on his sketching while traveling.

YOUTH & AGE

Caldecott enjoyed horses and riding. He often
incorporated them into his work.

Caldecott's activities or state of mind sometimes showed through in the drawings he made on his letters. He occasionally colored the drawings. Some of the sketches included hunting scenes, buildings, a formal dinner, or, in one case, himself stretched out on a couch. A line from the letter with the last sketch said "Too much exertion."

Caldecott spent much of his time with friends. The influence of Thomas Armstrong, his best friend and business associate, led Caldecott to develop an interest in art history and literature, particularly that of the 1700s. The interest helped Caldecott in his art. He and Armstrong saw each other nearly every day for business or pleasure, although they both thought that most of their business was also highly enjoyable.

Caldecott enjoyed social engagements as well as business engagements and often combined the two. In 1878, Caldecott commented to a "Miss M," who asked for his help in getting published, "Authors and their illustrators are seldom in unison; and often speak despitefully of one another. This is sad."

In 1879, Maria Mundella, daughter of A. J. Mundella, who was a member of Parliament and art patron, invited Caldecott to tea. In his acceptance letter dated July 23, he joked, "I shall be happy to take tea with you on Friday—even if there will be authoresses present." The "authoresses" who were present included Horatia Gatty, editor of *Aunt Judy's Magazine*, and Juliana Horatia Ewing, for whom Caldecott eventually illustrated three books.

In the autumn of 1878, Caldecott and Kate Greenaway, another illustrator for children, were weekend guests at the home of engraver Edmund Evans at Witley in Surrey. Mary Ann Evans, who wrote under the name "George Eliot," also attended the gathering.

In an October 1, 1878, letter to friend William Clough, Caldecott related an experience he had during that weekend at the Evans home. He said, "George Eliot, who lives at Witley, suggested that K.G. [Kate Greenaway] should go and see some twins at a neighbouring village. We drove on Sat. afternoon—a party—and 3 of us produced sketch-books and made a grand pencil charge upon the village. A history of the twins was kindly given by the mother, how they lived together, ate together, slept together, walked together, did everything together. Interesting. My opinion was that

Caldecott sketched three children he observed during a weekend
in the country in his friend Kate Greenaway's style.

they were 2 fat, ugly children who looked as though they
laid down to their food and slobbered it up. We all
thought them to be of the porcine genus."

That same weekend, Caldecott made a sketch of three
children in Greenaway's style. She kept the drawing for
the rest of her life.

Caldecott enjoyed life in the country. In the spring of
1875, he wrote to a friend saying, "I feel I owe some-
body an apology for staying the country too long, but
don't quite see to whom it is due, so I shall stay two or
three days longer, and then I shall indeed hang my harp
on a willow tree. It is difficult to screw up the proper
amount of courage for leaving the lambkins, the piglets,
the foals, the goslings, the calves, and the puppies."

While in the city, Caldecott missed the animals he
could have in the country. Caldecott enjoyed almost
every animal and child he met. Although the Caldecotts

never had children, Marian Caldecott became godmother to Thomas and Mary Armstrong's only son, who died before reaching adulthood.

Thomas Armstrong introduced Caldecott to artist Walter Crane and they also became friends. Crane said Caldecott often rode horseback to the Crane home in the early evenings. The primary purpose of Caldecott's visit was to play with Cranes' children before bedtime.

Children must have also liked Caldecott. Someone he had called upon in October 1878 described the visit by saying, "On the last evening of Mr. Caldecott's visit here, he was sitting at the dining-room table with the two little boys on his knees, and the rest of the family standing around him. . . ."

Caldecott loved most animals from the time he was a child, but he didn't like all of them. He once told Juliana Ewing, "I have time to add that of all dogs—all kinds of dogs—I think I have least sympathy with pugs. I have very little sympathy with the kind of human people they seem to me to represent in the doggy world."

Throughout most of his life, Caldecott had many pets, mostly horses and dogs. He mentioned some of his pets in a September 5, 1880, letter to friend William Clough saying, "We are quite well, I repeat, and so is the horse—barring a few of his feet (bit of 'thrush')—and the Russian pony (one Menschikoff by name—Menshakeoff [Men shake off], I mean it to be spelt and the dogs." At one time Caldecott also mentioned a dark chestnut mare named Peri.

Caldecott named one of his dogs, a dachshund, Lalla Rookh for a heroine of a poem by Tom Moore. Caldecott

And in that town a dog was found :
As many dogs there be —

Both mongrel,   puppy,   whelp,

and hound,

And curs of low degree.

Caldecott loved pets, especially horses and dogs. This illustration
is from his book, *Elegy on the Death of a Mad Dog*.

described Lalla as "an incorrigible fawner and jumper
about and begger." Lalla was the daughter of dogs
owned by Otto Weber and F. W. Keyl, both animal
painters. Queen Victoria once owned Lalla's mother.
According to Caldecott, Lalla's father "has often been to

Kensington Palace, and, I believe, Buckingham Palace also."

In 1881, Lalla had five puppies that Caldecott referred to as "Funny dogs!" One puppy named Topsy joined the family of Thomas Armstrong. Another puppy was promised to William Clough because, as Caldecott wrote to him in an August 11, 1881, letter, "Yours will be a happy home for any puppy." The puppy, named Brownie, died later that year. Caldecott said Clough "shall have another puppy whenever we can send one."

Caldecott wrote of the disappearance of Lalla in a November 16, 1884, letter to Clough. Caldecott said, "The mother of the pup I sent you—by name Lalla Rookh—disappeared 2 or 3 months ago. I had been exercising her after breakfast, and her son, and a beagle—Countess. While tying up Countess—Lalla went off with Toby—hunting in woods, I believe (we had to keep her up about that time on account of game adjacent). Toby returned 1 p.m. She never. Either smothered in rabbit-hole—or picked up by earliest arrivals of hop-pickers—a bad lot came to the neighbourhood of Farnham this year. Toby has since developed in intellect and friendliness. He converses at times with us."

Caldecott's delight in the world around him didn't stop at animals. One friend said, "His qualities were so bright, so new, so versatile, as to appeal at once to young and old. To a mind so singularly frank and open, and a shrewd but kindly humor, he united a rare grace and a delicate and refined sympathy which gave a distinctive and peculiar charm to all his artistic work; and to the po-

etic temperament with which he was also so richly en-
dowed by nature was added an enthusiastic enjoyment of
robust life, and a hearty liking for field sport."

Chapter Five

Art Studies and Habits

RANDOLPH CALDECOTT ATTENDED the Chester School of Art while still living with his father, stepmother, and siblings. After a year of art lessons, he learned all the instructor could teach him. The instructor suggested Caldecott practice to improve his skills. He happily practiced whenever he could.

After the Chester School of Art, Caldecott didn't receive further formal instruction until he moved to Manchester more than five years later. Upon arriving in Manchester, Caldecott immediately enrolled in evening classes at the Manchester School of Art. At the time, art classes focused on line drawing to prepare the artist for painting.

At the same time, Caldecott joined the Brasenose Club, an organization whose aim was "to promote the association of gentlemen of literary, scientific, or artistic professions, pursuits, or tastes." Caldecott spent many evenings at the Brasenose Club discussing art with the other members, some of whom also became friends. Seeing the work of the other members spurred Caldecott to copy his sketches in watercolors and practice modeling in clay.

The February 16, 1886, edition of the *Manchester Courier* told of Caldecott's death and discussed his life. A close friend was quoted as saying, "Whilst in this city [Manchester] so close was his application to the art that he loved that on several occasions he spent the whole night in drawing."

In May of 1870, Caldecott took some drawings to London to show Thomas Armstrong, a well-known artist at the time. A close friendship, as well as a business relationship, grew between Caldecott and Armstrong.

The visit whetted Caldecott's interest in London and the many opportunities for artists. Even with the Brasenose Club, Manchester didn't provide him with enough artistic opportunities. He saved money for two years while he worked on his portfolio. In 1872, Caldecott moved to London to pursue a career in art. He was prepared to go hungry to work on his art full time.

In London, Armstrong introduced Caldecott to many well-known artists such as James Whistler, Sir John Gilbert, and Thomas Lamont, all of whom Caldecott admired. It is unknown whether Caldecott ever met artist and illustrator George Du Maurier, whom Caldecott called "the greatest master of drawing in line that we have." Caldecott was also influenced by John Tenniel, known for his illustrations in *Alice's Adventures in Wonderland*, and John Leech, an illustrator for *Punch* from 1841 to 1864.

Famous artists of the time also admired Caldecott. Paul Gauguin said Caldecott's illustrations had "the true spirit of drawing." Vincent Van Gogh said, "Recently I saw a new edition of R. Caldecott's picture books and bought two of them, namely, illustrations of Washington Irving's Sketch Book. . . . Right now there are some people like Caldecott, for instance, who are quite original and highly interesting." Van Gogh also said, more simply, "Caldecott does such splendid work."

Editor Henry Blackburn introduced Caldecott to Sir Edward J. Poynter, a painter and member of the Royal Academy. Caldecott spent the two and one-half months from April 16 through June 29, 1872, enrolled in the Life Class Poynter taught at Slade Chair and School at the University College in London.

At one point, Caldecott met Jules Dalou, a French sculptor. Always ready for an opportunity to increase his artistic skills, Caldecott suggested they learn from each other. Dalou would teach Caldecott about clay modeling and Caldecott would help Dalou learn more of the English language.

While taking lessons from Monsieur Dalou, Caldecott completed two bas-reliefs under his guidance. A bas-relief is almost like a cross between a painting and a sculpture. The scene is carved against a flat surface. Caldecott called one bas-relief *The Boar Hunt* and the other, which was exhibited at the Royal Academy in 1878, he called *The Horse Fair in Brittany*.

Caldecott continued to work on his art while he studied. In a September 21, 1873, letter to a friend, he said ". . . for I am busy—not accumulating wealth, oh John, but wearing my life away in pursuit of fame and fortune. Gaze on this, shed a tear, & take another egg. I have four powerful blisters on my right hand now—Pheugh!"

Caldecott didn't limit himself to working in only one

Caldecott's drawing of himself showing his first work at the Royal Academy exhibition

type of media. In addition to his sketching, he sculpted in several different materials, painted with watercolors and oils, tried (and succeeded) in interior decoration, designed book plates, and experimented with chalk on brown paper.

Always seeking the way to create the best art, Caldecott also experimented with various kinds of ink. He wrote to illustrator Kate Greenaway on September 30, 1878, and gave her advice about using various kinds of ink. He said in his P.S., "I hope the above information may be of use to you."

Caldecott's interest in a variety of media carried over into his illustration techniques as well. Most of his illustrations were done using the wood engraving process, in which he would draw on paper and engravers transferred the lines to wood. He also worked with Dallastypes (using swelled gelatine to make photographic blocks) and the Dawson Typographic Etching Process, which Caldecott called "a fiendish process!" In the Dawson

Process, the illustrator used a needle to strip away a layer of wax coating a plate. Caldecott preferred the wood engraving process because drawing on paper gave him more freedom.

Caldecott's work with reproduction methods may have helped him create the excellent illustrations that he did. Henry Blackburn said, "Probably no English artist has benefited so much by the excellent reproductions of his drawings. He found out the secret very early in his career that the true way to work for reproduction was to be in sympathy with the engraver and colour printer."

Caldecott not only experimented with different types of media, but with different subjects as well. Whatever he drew, he tried to make the scene as accurate as possible. In a January 21, 1874, letter to his friend John Lennox, Caldecott said he was working on a large hunting drawing. He asked Lennox to loan him a pair of breeches for a fortnight "not to ride in" but "to draw from." He said, "I can get some here, but they won't do."

Caldecott took long walks in the city and sketched people, buildings, and waterfront scenes, but children and animals became his favorite subjects. He spent much of his time in London at the British Museum and the zoological gardens. Most of his serious work consisted of scenes in the country.

At one point, birds became Caldecott's favorite subject. He researched his work carefully by studying live birds as well as stuffed ones. On December 30, 1874, he asked an employee of the British Museum take the storks out of the cases. Caldecott could then study how the feathers grew on the wings from every angle.

Caldecott's forays into other art forms included this
sculpture of a cat ready to pounce.

Drawings of animals in Caldecott's sketch books include notations about how to correct them such as "front
hock like this" or "longer beak." Sketches of pigs and
parts of pigs (eyes, snouts, tails, hooves, etc.) overwhelm
one sketchbook. Twelve of these long and narrow black
notebooks are in the Caroline Miller Parker Collection in
the Houghton Library at the Harvard College Library.
Inside the front cover of the first sketch book dated
1872, Caldecott wrote

R. Caldecott, his book

46 Gt. Russell St. W C

In November of 1874, Caldecott began working on a
sculpture of a cat. To help his work, he used a cat skele-
ton, a dead cat, and a live cat as models. The sculpture
he finished on December 8 clearly shows the three
weeks of his study and effort. The cat, crouched and
ready to spring, looks as if it could come to life at any
moment.

Randolph Caldecott

Sometimes Caldecott needed a break from his hard work, as he showed in this illustration, "A Cool Sequestered Spot."

Caldecott's animals are very accurate. Edmund Evans, a friend and the engraver for the Picture Books, said, ". . . his cats, dogs, cows show how thoroughly he understood the anatomy of them."

Although Caldecott had a natural talent for drawing animals, he had difficulty drawing humans at first. He couldn't seem to make the size of head and limbs match the size of the body. One of the sketchbooks in the Parker Collection is filled with a variety of people in London from members of Parliament to cab drivers to women selling flowers. Hard work and practice helped him overcome the problem to his satisfaction.

Not everyone agreed. In an 1872 letter to the editor, Henry Blackburn at the time, one person criticized Caldecott's drawings of ladies in *London Society*. Caldecott took the criticism in stride. He drew a sketch of himself sitting in front of an easel and a woman model. In the sketch, Caldecott holds a chalice marked "Inspiration."

In another sketch, Caldecott drew himself near a table covered in empty wine bottles. The sketch was in answer to critics who said the quality of his work was suffering because he was drinking too much.

Caldecott usually accepted criticism well. He once wrote in reply to author Juliana Ewing, "It is however, a difficult thing to draw small faces in ink so that all observers shall agree to the age represented. . . . What you say of chins is true—I make a note of it—but the suggestion to 'give a touch more size to the eyes' makes one think one must be careful in accepting—or rather in acting upon—criticisms of this kind. Mr. Blackburn used to say that I was the only man who would alter—I like to do so when I am sure it would be better, although the certainty may be forced upon me by a critic who regards things with different eyes from mine."

While Caldecott accepted criticism well, he could also be critical of others. In a July 31, 1879, letter to Horatia Gatty, editor of *Aunt Judy's Magazine*, he said, "It is just possible that you may see the summer number of the *Graphic*. Therein is a series of illustrations by me, and the letterpress accompanying—bearing the frivolous title of *Flirtations in France*—is also attributed to me— bearing my initials—but I am not responsible for the last 40 odd lines containing one or two *dreadful* remarks and jokes—these were added instead of my winding up short sentences—to fill up the page. It is not an important matter to the world at large: but I should be sorry that any friends of mine credited me with what I object to."

Although he didn't think of himself as a writer, Caldecott often changed or added to the text. Always the perfectionist, he was careful about the changes he made. In discussing the changes to writing, he said, "As regards the misuse of certain words, I consult the authorities when a doubt crossed my mind, and I find with sorrow,

Caldecott used life experiences for many sketches.

in which I am joined by other anxious spirits, that the English language is being ruined, chiefly by journalists, English and American."

Caldecott appreciated favorable reviews and comments from others. In a letter to friend and fellow bank clerk William Clough on May 13, 1881, he said, ". . . for I do like a touch of well-worded praise. I think that I *may* deserve it."

Many people admired Caldecott's depictions of people. After Juliana Ewing asked him about his seeming to avoid drawing military subjects, Caldecott responded in a December 4, 1881, letter saying, "I do not dislike military subjects—it is only that military people are not generally remarkable for strength of head."

Most people were happy to pose for Caldecott when

he asked, even they didn't speak the same language. Henry Blackburn said that when Caldecott worked on *The Harz Mountains: A Tour in the Toy Country*, "The interviews were conducted slowly and gravely, ending in peals of laughter from the natives."

Caldecott enjoyed drawing caricatures. On July 9, 1872, he wrote he had been "engaged on chalk caricatures all day." When someone once asked Caldecott to draw portraits for an album, he refused in fear that "some touch of caricature or keen insight should hurt any one of them." In a February 3, 1883, response to friend Frederick Green, who asked him to paint a portrait of his wife, Caldecott wrote, "I fear that I ought not to approach Mrs. Green brush in hand—my brush is not a very reverent one."

Caldecott even poked fun at himself in some of his work. He drew himself as the sick father in the Picture Book *The Babes in the Wood*. Most people in his illustrations seem to be bursting with health and energy—the opposite of his own delicate health.

Ill health didn't keep Caldecott from wandering around the city looking for scenes to sketch. While in London, he often went to the Houses of Parliament to sketch the members and the groups that gathered around them.

Any public gathering such as new play openings or weddings Caldecott attended would likely turn into several drawings in his sketchbook. In an October 22, 1873, letter to friend William Etches, Caldecott said, "I heard Mark Twain lecture the other day. It was very hearable. He says lots of dry and humorous things." Of course,

Caldecott sketched the American author.

Caldecott also searched rural areas for scenes to sketch. While living in the country, he spent much of his time walking, riding, and hunting in the area. Managing the farm he purchased took some of his time away from his art, but he found that type of work greatly satisfying. Because the farm didn't produce much income, he had to keep working on his art to survive.

Most of the time Caldecott's schedule consisted of spending the mornings working indoors, the afternoons outdoors, and the evenings working on correspondence. Caldecott wrote in a January 7, 1883, letter to author Edwin Waugh, "The truth is—and I always prefer the truth when practicable and troubleless—my business (!) correspondence leaves me no time for the feast—which I always feel it to be—of writing to a friend."

Caldecott's wife, Marian, wrote to Juliana Ewing in her November 3, 1884, letter, "I have always wished, and used to hope that I might sometimes act as secretary to him, but he is more particular than anyone I know, and has always said that it is less trouble to him to do it himself."

Sketches, often humorous, adorned most of Caldecott's outgoing mail. The sketches often showed what was going on in his life at the time. Many of his letters also had an illustration including a sign, flag, ribbon, or other means in which he could incorporate his address at the top.

In addition to personal and business mail, Caldecott also answered fan mail. Some people sent him their artwork for him to critique. Caldecott tried to answer them as honestly as he could. In an 1874 letter to a six-year-old, Caldecott wrote, "I thank you very much for your grand sheet of drawings, which I think are very nice indeed. I hope you will go on trying and learning to draw. There are many beautiful things waiting to be drawn. Animals and flowers oh! such a many—and a few people."

Caldecott often used what he considered his "bad" drawings as packing material around his correspondence. In an August 22, 1882, letter to William Clough, he said, "This is an important letter so I pack it with some rough protective stuff." The "rough protective stuff" consisted of work Caldecott considered inadequate.

Caldecott had plenty of "packing material." He rarely corrected his illustrations, but simply started over from scratch. Engraver Edmund Evans said, "If the sketches came all right—he let them pass—if he was not satisfied with the results, he generally tore them up and burned them."

Evans said the first sketches, called "Lightning Sketches," Caldecott made in the development of a project "were little more than outlines, but they were so racy and spontaneous."

Even his finished illustrations, especially those in the latter part of his career, have few lines. Reviewer W. E. Henly said in the November 16, 1878, *Academy*, "Mr. Caldecott is of the rare artists who never waste a stroke, who give you in a dozen scratches the effect that some men fail to produce by an elaborate system of composition and design."

Although Caldecott's sketches tend to look relatively

quick to complete, he spent a great deal of time on each one. Caldecott was a perfectionist; each line had to be perfect on something as large as a full-page spread or as small as a simple action sketch.

Caldecott's sparse sketches cut down the possibility of error. As he often said, "The fewer the lines, the less error committed." He also considered "the art of leaving out as a science."

Excess lines aren't the only thing Caldecott left out of many of his drawings. If he signed his work at all, he usually used only his initials. Even the initials are often difficult to spot since they are usually incorporated into a section of the drawing. He may have been partially following the example of Walter Crane, who used a rebus to sign his illustrations.

Caldecott said in an August 15, 1877, letter to wood engraver James Davis Cooper, ". . . as for myself I would rather leave out my initials than to have them interfere with the drawing—and I often do—and in these slight drawings every little tells."

Soon Caldecott's success brought him more work than he could easily handle. He became so busy with illustrating, he had little time for serious painting. Luckily, he thought that ". . . plenty of work to engage the attention makes any sort of a day slip by only too quickly."

Occasionally, Caldecott found himself easily distracted from his work. While in Menton, he wrote to Jane Locker-Lampson on January 11, 1879. He said, "I fled yesterday from Cannes, which—although called a very quiet place by most visitors—I found to be too lively for one who has much work to do and a desire to do it."

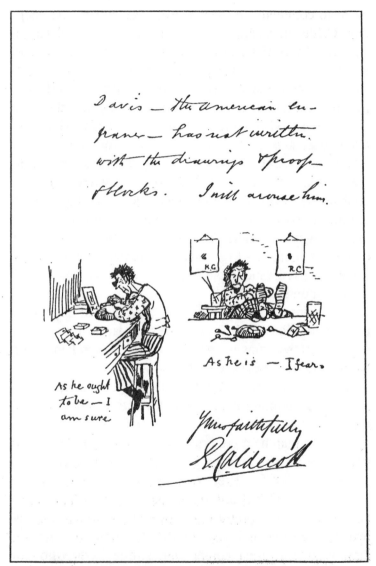

Caldecott's sketch of himself during a rare time when he wasn't enthusiastic about his work.

At times even having enthusiasm for his art was difficult for him. In a May 19, 1880, letter to friend Frederick
Locker-Lampson, Caldecott included a sketch of himself
working. The caption read, "As he ought to be—I am
sure." Another sketch showed him leaning back with his
feet on a desk. That caption said, "As he is—I fear."

Caldecott rarely turned down work, especially at the
beginning of his art career. The overwork and his ill
health caused him to become more and more tired. He
once said, "I'm getting awfully tired of winter with its
cold winds, and I shall hail the advent of spring with a
joy unspeakable. Naturally belonging to the class of human beings denominated 'lazy,' I can't bear have to
move about fast to keep warm. I like 'to lay all work
aside and stretch me in the sun and dream, &c,' as one of
the later poets saith."

The more tired he became, the less pleased Caldecott
became with his work. The images on paper simply did-
n't match the images in his mind. He worked even
harder and became more tired. His wife, Marian, became
concerned and asked him to slow down, but his work
ethic made him want to honor the agreements he had
made.

Even though he often criticized his own art, Caldecott
prided himself on being a good business manager. In a
January 17, 1875, letter to a former coworker at the
Manchester and Salford Bank, he said, "I stick pretty
close to business, pretty much in that admirable and at-
tentive manner which was the delight, the pride, the ex-
ultation of the great chiefs who strode it through the
Manchester banking halls. Yes, I have not forsaken those

gay—though perhaps, to the heart yearning to be fetter-less, irksome—scenes without finding that the world ever requires toil from those sons of labour who would be successful."

Caldecott's bank training provided a good back-ground for the financial side of his art career. He set the fees for his work fairly. His logic told him that if he put less work into a project, he could accept a smaller pay-ment.

Caldecott summed up his approach to art in an August 27, 1873, letter to friend John Harrison. Caldecott said, "You know how devoted I was to business when I was a quill-driver; well, now I am still more devoted, and hope by a strict attention to business and by still sup-plying the best article at the lowest price to merit a con-tinuance of the favours which the nobility, clergy, &c."

Chapter Six

The Fine Art Career

RANDOLPH CALDECOTT LIKELY would have appreciated being able to make a living from his art, particularly the fine arts, from the time he finished school. He probably didn't think that was possible because few people are able to make their living in the arts. Instead, he settled into his work at the Whitchurch and Ellesmere Bank.

Caldecott continued to work on his art whenever he could. After moving to Manchester, the opportunities to pursue his art increased. His membership in the Brasenose Club helped him both with his art and in developing friendships with other artists.

James Blower, another clerk at the Manchester and Salford Bank, realized how much talent Caldecott had and suggested he exhibit his art. When members of the Brasenose Club asked him to join their exhibition, Caldecott happily agreed.

Caldecott exhibited his work for the first time at the Royal Manchester Institution in 1869. The primary piece at his exhibition was *At the Wrong End of the Wood*, a hunting frieze painted in white on brown paper. He also included a few other paintings and sketches of both country and city life. Caldecott's art received excellent reviews.

In 1872, Caldecott moved to London to pursue his art career full time. Since he needed money, he took almost any job offered. In a January 1, 1874, letter to friend William Etches, Caldecott said, "I have just got a new workshop next door at the back, and there I light my stove and carry on my business." He went on to joke, "Do you want a sign-board? or an equestrian statue? or an elegant wallpaper?"

The comment wasn't entirely a joke. During his first year in London, Caldecott often worked on interior decoration, many projects as part of friend and business associate Thomas Armstrong's work. Caldecott once painted decorative panels for author and artist Henry Renshaw's home. The wealthy Renshaw called his home Bank House, located at Chapel-en-le-Frith.

Although he would have preferred to work on his paintings and other fine art, Caldecott took the interior design job seriously. The project took many months to complete because he researched birds thoroughly to make sure details were accurate.

Caldecott also designed four columns with peacock decorations for the Arab room at the home of accomplished painter Lord Frederic Leighton. Artist Walter Crane designed a tiled peacock frieze for the same room.

During his first years in London, Caldecott also worked on many paintings for friends. Hunting scenes dominated most of these paintings. Many of his hunting scenes in oil also appeared at an exhibition at the Royal Manchester Institution in March 1872.

Caldecott's oil paintings were not as popular as his watercolors, which were highly praised. He was elected

One of Caldecott's oil paintings, *The Three Huntsmen.*

to the Royal Institute of Watercolour Painting in 1872.

Members of the Royal Academy urged Caldecott to spend more time on his paintings. At first he thought he didn't have enough training and needed the income from illustrations. Later he decided he liked the fame and increasing money that illustrating brought him.

Caldecott continued to work on his fine art and tried new mediums. He once wrote to a friend, "Save up and be an art patron; you will soon be able to buy some interesting terra cottas by R. C.!"

Caldecott also produced other types of art. Editor Henry Blackburn was asked to make a presentation before the Society of Arts in London in March 1875. He, in turn, asked Caldecott to do a series of diagrams on the power of line and effects to be gained by simple methods of illustration for a paper titled "The Art of Illustration." Caldecott did a diagram seven-feet tall and five-feet wide of two horses called "Youth and Age," as well as several other diagrams, all on the same large scale.

During his career, Caldecott produced at least two alphabets. One is a "sporting" alphabet with hunting, fishing, boating, swimming, and other activities to illustrate each letter of the alphabet. The other alphabet featured humorous and fanciful scenes.

In 1876, Caldecott displayed two pieces of artwork at the Royal Academy exhibition. The bas-relief, *The Horse Fair in Brittany*, received more attention than the painting *There were Three Ravens sat on a Tree*, probably because the painting was hung in a bad place.

A reviewer in the June 10, 1876, edition of the *Saturday Review* said, "Of low relief—taking the Elgin frieze as the standard—one of the purest examples we have seen for many a day is Mr. Caldecott's bas-relief, 'A Horse Fair in Brittany.' Here a simple and almost rude incident in nature has been brought within the laws and symmetry of art."

Another exhibition at the Royal Academy in 1878 gave Caldecott his first serious attention as a painter. Two of his similar oil paintings, *The Three Huntsmen* and *The Three Jovial Huntsmen*, later became the basis for a Picture Book published in 1880.

As with *There were Three Ravens Sat on a Tree* two years earlier, Caldecott didn't like where *The Three Huntsmen* was placed. In a May 3, 1878, letter to friend

Randolph Caldecott

Caldecott's painting, "The Three Jovial Huntsmen," served as inspiration for a children's book of the same name. This illustration is from the book published in 1880.

William Clough, Caldecott complained about the positioning of the painting. He said, "I have a picture there—oh, so dreadfully, dreadfully hung! Too high for the interesting details to be discovered and so opposed in tone and key to the picture below it that all the many charms of its effect and general aspect have faded like the tracery of frost. So badly placed it is and so sad and looks that I won't make a sketch for Academy Notes (Blackburn's) although desired."

A. J. Mundella, the member of the parliament for Sheffield, bought the painting *The Three Huntsmen*, not from the exhibition, but in Mundella's words "from his easel." Mundella's granddaughter later became the model for the young Queen in the Picture Book *Sing a Song for Sixpence*.

At one point, the Royal Mint hired Caldecott to design a campaign medal for those who fought in the Second Afghanistan War campaign for years 1878-1880. Leonard Charles Wyon, Chief Engraver to the Royal Mint, engraved the Afghanistan War campaign medal from Caldecott's design. The medal's ribbon was usually green with a crimson stripe at each edge, although the colors sometimes varied. The back of the medal, designed entirely by Caldecott, featured soldiers, horses, an elephant, and a gun. The front of the medal showed an image of Queen Victoria designed by Sir Joachim Boehm. The queen originally objected to that likeness of her because it showed her as an older woman. Most of the stamps and coins featured her as she looked when she was 18.

In 1880, Caldecott became a member of the Manchester Academy of Fine Arts.

Caldecott's fine art didn't give him the same fame as his illustrations, probably because fewer people were able to see it and even fewer were able to afford to have pieces of original artwork in their homes.

Caldecott didn't forget his family or his home town while pursuing his career. He provided artwork for an 1883 charity exhibition in Chester. Before the exhibition, Caldecott wrote to E. J. Baillie, who organized the exhibition, with a special request. Caldecott asked that his stepmother and her three daughters (likely Caldecott's half-sisters), who lived at 19 Pepper Street at the time, be given free admission to the event. Caldecott's father had died in 1875.

Caldecott's fine art has been displayed in more than

twenty exhibitions in galleries including Dudley Gallery, The Fine Art Society, the Grosvenor Gallery, the Institute of Painters in Water Colour, the Royal Academy, and the Royal Manchester Institution, among others.

After Caldecott's death, his estate catalog listed forty-one "finished pictures and studies in oil" and twelve different sculptures in bronze, plaster, and wax. The Fine Art Society handled the sale of most of the fine art sold while Caldecott was alive. The Victoria and Albert Museum in London has 259 of Caldecott's pictures and seven of his sketchbooks.

In his short lifetime, Caldecott completed at least 56 oil paintings and 22 sculptures. He also published illustrations in at least 66 books and more than 120 illustrations in at least 14 different periodicals. Obviously Caldecott's art was his life. Even though Caldecott was more well-known for his work in illustrating, he was an accomplished fine artist as well.

Chapter Seven

The Illustrating Career

IN NOVEMBER 1861, soon after Randolph Caldecott began working at Whitchurch and Ellesmere Bank, he visited his family in Chester. The Queen Railway Hotel (now called the Queen's Hotel) burned during his visit. The Caldecott family went to City Road opposite the railroad station to see the fire.

Naturally, Caldecott sketched the fire. Because photography was not perfected at the time, newspapers needed drawings of the fire. Caldecott submitted his sketch, along with an article describing the fire, to the *Illustrated London News*. The drawing appeared in the December 7, 1861, issue. Caldecott received the first payment for his art at age fifteen.

Randolph Caldecott's brother Alfred asked him why he didn't sign the drawing. Caldecott said he didn't think the picture would be printed. Caldecott agreed to sign his drawings from then on, but only with his initials. He usually signed his art, but if he thought his initials would interfere with the look of the scene, he refused to add even his initials.

Caldecott became somewhat of a celebrity. His co-workers at the bank went out of their way to congratulate him. Customers stopped at the bank just to see him. The fame didn't last long. Caldecott had to wait nearly seven years before his next publication.

Finally, Caldecott sold another sketch. This time his work appeared in the July 1868 issue of *Will o' the Wisp*. The drawing featured a young boy holding a copy of the newspaper. Other humorous publications, given human features, stared at the boy in amazement.

Caldecott's art at the 1869 exhibition at the Royal Manchester Institution received excellent reviews. The reviews spurred him to send some sketches to *The Sphinx*. Caldecott's work began appearing regularly in *The Sphinx* and other magazines and newspapers. The job at the bank soon took second place in importance to him.

In May 1870, Caldecott took some sketches to London. He met with Thomas Armstrong, an established artist and the art director of the South Kensington Museum.

Caldecott collected some of his drawings in a book he called "Fancies of a Wedding." The drawings greatly impressed Armstrong. He asked to keep the sketches to show to Henry Blackburn, the editor of a popular magazine called *The London Society*. Blackburn bought several of the sketches for his magazine. The payment for the first batch of drawings was £30—about three months' salary at the bank.

Blackburn soon asked Caldecott to provide illustrations in connection with the text of a story. His illustration for the story "The Two Trombones," written by ac-

Caldecott's Illustration, "The Two Trombones", from *London Society*, 1871.

tor F. Robson, appeared in the Christmas 1871 issue of *London Society*.

Armstrong introduced Caldecott to Mark Lemon, editor of *Punch*. Lemon examined a small drawing in wood and "Fancies of a Wedding." Caldecott later said, "From that day to this, I have not seen either sketch or book." None of the drawings are known to have appeared in print, despite Lemon's promise that at least one would. Several other of his illustrations were eventually published in *Punch*, the first in the June 22, 1872, issue.

Henry Blackburn noticed that Caldecott could sketch quickly. Blackburn suggested he try illustrating stories for newspapers. Whenever a story happened, day or night, Caldecott had to be there. He also had to complete a drawing immediately after finishing a sketch, when he preferred to have time to think before starting an illustration. He also noticed that his landscapes suffered in the reproduction process. The stress of deadlines also had a bad effect on his health. Even with all the drawbacks associated with newspaper illustration, Caldecott enjoyed the work.

Caldecott continued to publish in magazines and newspapers throughout his career. In addition to *Will o' the Wisp* and *The Sphinx*, his illustrations appeared in *Punch*, *The Pictorial World*, and *Graphic*, among others. In addition to many illustrations for several issues of *Aunt Judy's Magazine*, Caldecott also designed the cover of the November 1881 issue. The February 1884 issue of *English Illustrated Magazine* carried Caldecott's illustrations for Robert Louis Stevenson's story, "The Character of Dogs."

Caldecott often adjusted the writing to his personal use and even occasionally wrote entire verses to sell with his illustrations. Sometimes editors rejected his illustrations because they poked too much fun at high society and politicians.

Lack of money continued to be a problem. Even with all the work he had, Caldecott still needed more income. In the summer of 1872, he wrote to Henry Blackburn and said, "Florence Marryat wants me to illustrate a novelette, very humorous, to run through five or six numbers of *London Society*, beginning in February . . . I think I shall do them, I want coin!"

Meeting the deadlines for newspapers and magazines became a problem, especially after Caldecott's health began to worsen. Some critics suggested that alcohol could have been part of the problem since the quality of his work also seemed to deteriorate.

Blackburn thought that Caldecott's heart really wasn't in illustrating for magazines and newspapers even though "his powers seemed eminently fitted." Hoping to give him another way of earning a living as well as possibly easing Caldecott's health problems, Blackburn suggested he illustrate books instead. Books required less pressure than magazines. Also, illustrating travel books would allow Caldecott to spend winters in warmer climates.

Blackburn decided to write a book about the Harz Mountains in Europe and hired Caldecott to do the illustrations. Caldecott spent a year traveling with Mr. and Mrs. Blackburn while they worked on the project.

While on the trip, Caldecott carried an English/German translation dictionary with him wherever he went. He said the translation guide made it difficult for him to find the words he needed, and at the same time had too many phrases that were "elaborate and quite unnecessary." He enjoyed talking with the people of Harz even with the language difficulties.

At the end of a year, Caldecott had a portfolio of sketches. He returned to London looking and feeling much healthier.

The book, *The Harz Mountains: A Tour in the Toy Country*, became Caldecott's first book, published by Sampson Low, Marston, Low & Searle in 1873. Caldecott provided 27 of the 40 illustrations in the book.

The Harz Mountains gave most Americans their first chance to see Caldecott's work through excerpts that appeared in the June 1873 issue of *Harper's New Monthly Journal* and the September 16, 1873, issue of the New York *Daily Graphic*. Caldecott was called "London Artistic Correspondent" for the New York *Daily Graphic*.

Plans for a translation of "Harz" into German came to a halt when German officials thought Caldecott had caricatured well-known people in his illustrations. He hadn't, but his natural style made the portrayals look like cartoons.

In January 1873, publisher George Routledge & Sons released *Frank Mildmay or The Naval Officer* by Captain Marryat. The book is believed to be the first book Caldecott illustrated for children. The company, now called Frederick Warne & Company, which is now a division of Viking Penguin, later published Caldecott's Picture Books. Edmund Evans, who engraved the Picture Books, also engraved the illustrations for *Frank Mildmay*.

In 1874 and 1875, Caldecott worked on the illustrations for a collection of some of Aesop's fables his brother Alfred translated. Engraver James Cooper insisted Caldecott do the illustrations set in the current time. Randolph used himself as a model for many of the illustrations.

Some of Aesop's Fables with Modern Instances, not published until 1883, wasn't successful, possibly because the public thought the illustrations looked too contemporary when they expected "old-fashioned" characters and scenes.

Caldecott, himself, was disappointed in "Aesop." He said, "Do not expect much from this book. When I see

Some of

Æsop's Fables.

With " Modern Instances."

Shown in designs by R. CALDECOTT.

"Aesop's Fables" was a collaboration between Caldecott and his brother Alfred.

LONDON :
MACMILLAN AND CO.
1883.

proofs of it I wonder and regret that I did not approach the subject more seriously."

Soon after Caldecott returned from Harz, engraver James Cooper hired Caldecott to illustrate *Old Christmas: Selections from The Sketch Book* by Washington Irving. Cooper said the publication of Irving's book had "been delayed in execution for many years, mainly from the difficulty of finding an artist capable of identifying himself with the author."

Critics praised Caldecott's illustrations in *Old Christmas.*

Several publishers disagreed with Cooper's choice of artist and declined to publish the work. One editor called Caldecott's drawings "inartistic, flippant, vulgar and unworthy of the author of *Old Christmas.*" Finally an editor at Macmillan recognized Caldecott's talent and published the book in 1875.

Reviewers praised Caldecott's 120 black-and-white illustrations for the book. One reviewer said, "Washington Irving's *Old Christmas* was made alive for us by a new interpreter, who brought grace of drawing with a dainty inventive genius to the delineation of English life in the last century." The favorable reviews were so numerous that Caldecott drew a sketch of himself falling asleep hearing Cooper reading the reviews praising *Old Christmas*. The success of the book helped Caldecott get much more work.

In 1875, Caldecott's illustrations appeared in the book *Baron Bruno or the Unbelieving Philosopher and other Fairy Stories* by Louisa Morgan. The stories are similar to the Brothers Grimm fairy tales. The illustrations are darker and more crowded with details than those in the unique style he later developed.

In 1876, Macmillan released *Bracebridge Hall,* also by Washington Irving. Caldecott provided 116 illustrations for that book. Caldecott gave James Cooper, who also engraved these illustrations, equal credit for the success of *Bracebridge Hall.*

Caldecott used pen and ink to do the initial drawings for *Bracebridge Hall.* He drew them about one-third larger than the those that appeared in the book. His drawings were photographed on wood, then engraved in facsimile. Lack of margins in the first editions spoiled the effect of many of the final illustrations. *Old Christmas* and *Bracebridge Hall* were soon combined in one volume.

Caldecott provided 28 illustrations for *North Italian Folk: Sketches of Town and Country Life* by Mrs. Comyns Carr, published by Chatto and Windus in 1878. The author was the wife of J. W. Comyns Carr, the editor of *The English Illustrated Magazine*, for whom Caldecott provided illustrations. The illustrations in *North Italian Folk* were colored by hand. An advance copy Caldecott gave to his sister Sophia in 1877 doesn't have the color added.

The illustrations for *North Italian Folk* didn't receive much attention. Henry Blackburn thought Caldecott's work and style had become too identified with English people. Also, Mrs. Comyns Carr had so skillfully woven details into the text of the book that Caldecott couldn't add much to the illustrations.

Blackburn asked Caldecott to do a series of illustrations of Britain's castles, cathedrals, and other buildings in 1878. Caldecott "did not take to this idea" because, besides enjoying the process of drawing live subjects more, he didn't think he drew inanimate objects as well.

In late 1878, George Routledge & Sons released the first two of Caldecott's Picture Books, *The House that Jack Built* and *The Diverting History of John Gilpin*. Although Caldecott and engraver Edmund Evans hoped the Picture Books would do well, they didn't realize that the Picture Books would become the primary means by which Caldecott is remembered.

Association with Juliana Horatia Ewing

In 1879, Caldecott met Juliana Horatia Ewing, a respected children's author. Her mother, Margaret Gatty, founded *Aunt Judy's Magazine*. Ewing and her sister, Horatia Gatty, later edited the magazine.

Illustration from *The House that Jack Built,* one
of Caldecott's first picture books.

Ewing wanted Caldecott to illustrate a book for her,
but he was too busy at first. He did have time to provide
a color illustration for the story "Jackanapes" in *Aunt
Judy's Magazine*. He didn't have a chance to read the
story before he did the illustration, but drew from Ewing's instructions.

By the time his other work eased up enough so that
Caldecott was able to illustrate Ewing's books, the two
had become friends. They had something in common
besides their creative pursuits: both of them suffered
from ill health.

The first major project Caldecott and Ewing did together was the story "Jackanapes" expanded to book
length. The two controlled the production of *Jackanapes*
until bound copies were delivered to the publisher, the

Society for the Promotion of Christian Knowledge.

At the time of *Jackanapes*, Ewing had written many more books than Caldecott had illustrated, but Caldecott was more successful. When Ewing expressed her fear that she wasn't a good enough writer for him to illustrate her work, Caldecott wrote in a December 5, 1882, letter to her, "You must not *think*—let alone *say*—that your work does not please me or 'attract' me. If you knew with what avidity I seized upon *Laetus sorte meâ* and how I express myself about your writing when I ever have a chance you would not so misunderstand me. The truth is—I have such an opinion of your force that I feel timid about illustrating you." Obviously, Caldecott highly respected her ability.

Caldecott acted almost like an agent for Ewing as to production details, estimates, and royalties. In a December 19, 1882, letter to her, he said, "Do not think I do not consider the author's deserts [Note that Caldecott spelled "desserts" wrong.]. I look upon the author as removed from the baser herd of printers, paper-makers, binders, packers, illustrators, and publishers who must be paid as tradesmen. An author is much above that sort of thing— except in profits (as a rule) and in these the deserving author *should* be pre-eminent always."

As for his own royalties, Caldecott told Ewing in a March 7, 1883, letter, "The 3½d after 10,000 would not allow me any royalty: but I do not want much beyond being associated with you in any success the book may have."

At first Caldecott must have worried that he wouldn't make much money on the book. The initial copies of

Jackanapes were published with "dull stone-colored paper colors" and didn't sell well. When the books were reissued in colorful paper covers, they became a huge success. The first 2,000 copies of *Jackanapes* in paper covers sold within two weeks.

Ewing wanted to work on another book with Caldecott. In an October 1884 letter, she said, ". . . if my best and tersest and most finished writing combined in one volume with our finest and freest work, such as in the best of your toybooks, we might command a success that would make haggling over a few pounds for engraving worse than folly."

Their next book, *Daddy Darwin's Dovecot,* created difficulties and disappointments for Caldecott. Edmund Evans, the printer for that book as well as the others on which Caldecott and Ewing collaborated, made a mistake and printed the book in black ink instead of the brown Caldecott preferred. The poor quality of etching and faulty electrotypes produced many errors in the illustrations that the black ink emphasized.

After getting copies of *Daddy Darwin's Dovecot,* Caldecott wrote to Evans on November 5, 1884, to mention his concerns—tactfully, of course. He said, "Printing does seem to me a puzzle—because the appearance of the illustrations in the book is different from the proofs. If I had known that the process blocks would not have printed clearer I should have begged for your old-fashioned wood engraving." Despite all that, he included an afterthought saying, "Mrs. R. C. says D.D.D. is a 'lovely little book!'"

Caldecott commented about Evans in a January 22,

DADDY DARWIN'S
DOVECOT

A Country Tale by
JULIANA HORATIA EWING
Author of
JACKANAPES
&c.

ILLUSTRATED
BY
RANDOLPH
CALDECOTT

LONDON:
SOCIETY FOR PROMOTING CHRISTIAN KNOWLEDGE,
NORTHUMBERLAND AVENUE, CHARING CROSS, W.C.;
BRIGHTON: 135, NORTH STREET.
NEW YORK: E. AND J. B. YOUNG AND CO.

Caldecott's collaboration with Juliana Horatia Ewing proved
to be successful, if short lived.

1884, letter to Ewing. He said, "I fear that he does not attend closely enough to the details—or to the carrying-out of details—of the work which he undertakes."

For their next book, *Lob-Lie-by-the-Fire*, Caldecott and Ewing went back to wood-engraved illustrations. After Ewing became too ill to continue the business associated with the book, her sister, Horatia Gatty, worked with Caldecott. Ewing died on May 13, 1885, at age 43. She never saw the finished book. Had she lived, she and Caldecott likely would have collaborated on at least one more book before Caldecott's death the following year. People said that, because Caldecott's and Ewing's deaths occurred less than a year apart, "they have gone to Heaven together."

Caldecott's respect for Ewing can be seen in his October 13, 1885, letter to Gatty commenting on her memoir of Ewing. He said, "I need not say that I have been much interested in your Memoir of Mrs Ewing. There are certain things therein mentioned which I regret that I did not know before. I feel sure that the memoir will be appreciated in many quarters." The Society for the Protection of Christian Knowledge published *Juliana Horatia Ewing and Her Books* in 1885.

In 1880, Caldecott had 170 illustrations published in Henry Blackburn's book *Breton Folk: An Artistic Tour in Brittany*. Three of the illustrations include Caldecott himself. One illustration is of him leaning against a wall in a ballroom watching people dance; another is of him sitting on a curb in front of an iron fence and children around him; and one is of his back as he watches the people gamble in a

Caldecott was kept working hard as an illustrator. *Breton Folk* alone contained 170 of his illustrations.

Breton Folk.

With One Hundred and Seventy Illustrations

by R. CALDECOTT.

LONDON:
SAMPSON LOW, MARSTON, SEARLE, & RIVINGTON,
CROWN BUILDINGS, 188, FLEET STREET.
1880.

game room in Monte Carlo. The illustrations are now in the Victoria and Albert Museum in London.

Caldecott continued to illustrate books in the years that followed. He kept his sense of humor. The back of the title page of the *A Sketch-Book of R. Caldecott's*, released in 1883, has a special note in Caldecott's handwriting. The message states, "Dedicated to everybody—but copyright reserved."

Edmund Evans, who engraved the book, said, "The

Sketch-Book was not a success—why, I could never understand." Some people said the book, which concerned the four seasons, fell between two types of readers. Although generally appearing to be for children, the satire may have been too difficult for children to understand. Whatever the reason, *A Sketch-Book of R. Caldecott's* was one of his rare works that was not entirely successful.

Had Caldecott lived longer, he likely would have worked with Charles Lutwidge Dodgson, author of *Alice's Adventures in Wonderland* under the pen name Lewis Carroll. Dodgson wrote in his diary on February 4, 1883, "Heard from Mr Caldecott who would like to draw for me, but is too deeply engaged to undertake anything at present. I must try and engage him for some future time, and could then feel encouraged to work definitely at a new book." Many people wished they could have seen the results of such a collaboration.

Edmund Evans suggested Caldecott and Kate Greenaway collaborate on William Mavor's *English Spelling Book*. Caldecott did a preliminary drawing for the book and Greenaway designed a cover with both their names on it. Later, Greenaway decided she didn't want to collaborate and did the book alone in 1885.

Caldecott was a little over a year old when Evans had completed learning his trade as an engraver. The shrewd businessman noticed the rising interest in books and children's books in particular. He printed books in red and blue ink on white paper. The white covers dirtied quickly and didn't sell well. Evans changed to shiny yellow paper. The books, nicknamed "yellow backs" or "mustard plasters," did sell well. Evans hired Caldecott to do that type of book after illustrator Walter Crane became busy with other projects.

Evans once worked with Kate Greenaway's father John. Evans also worked with many other illustrators including Kate Greenaway and Walter Crane, both of whom weren't well known until their association with Evans. Greenaway's "prettier" and more child-like illustrations were likely more popular than Caldecott's illustrations at the time. Caldecott's talent was in adding details to stories through his illustrations.

At the time of his death, Caldecott was working on *Jack and the Beanstalk*, written by Hallam Tennyson, son of Alfred, Lord Tennyson. Evans used Caldecott's initial sketches for that book, published in 1886. The illustrations don't appear to be as "finished" as those in his other books. *Jack and the Beanstalk* was not intended to be one of the Picture Books. "Jack" has 70 pages instead of the approximately 30 pages of the Picture Books. The book is also of a smaller size. The book was published by Macmillan instead of Routledge.

Although Caldecott is known primarily for his Picture Books, the illustrations he did for other books and periodicals deserve to be recognized as well. As Joseph Pennell, American etcher and book illustrator, said "There is no one in England who has ever equaled him . . . and I very much doubt if any one anywhere ever surpassed him."

Chapter Eight

The Picture Books

WHEN RANDOLPH CALDECOTT was a child, books had illustrations that were either hand-colored or printed by methods that gave poor results. By the time Caldecott began illustrating, methods had improved greatly, but he did something different in style. At the time, most illustrators did one illustration per page, but Caldecott often had several illustrations per page to add more details to the story and characterizations that weren't a part of the text.

Several "toy books" Walter Crane illustrated for engraver Edmund Evans sold well. Eventually, Crane became too busy designing wallpaper for wealthy people to illustrate the toy books. Evans searched for another children's book illustrator to continue illustrating that type of books. He noticed Caldecott's illustrations in *Old Christmas*.

Caldecott's illustrations inspired Evans to ask Caldecott to illustrate books of folk songs and nursery rhymes for children's books. They called the books "Picture Books" to distinguish them from the "toy books," although Caldecott's books are sometimes called "Caldecott toy books."

Caldecott went to see Walter Crane and ask for advice. Crane suggested Caldecott ask for a set amount of money for each book sold instead of a flat fee. Caldecott asked Evans for a penny a copy for each book sold. That penny is now called an "old penny" and had twelve pence to a shilling at the time instead of the five pence to a shilling today.

Evans refused to consider the offer at first. Caldecott argued that he would receive nothing if the books didn't sell. After a long and sometimes angry discussion, Evans agreed to pay all costs of producing the books and Caldecott would get a penny a copy. Caldecott became one of the first people, if not the first person, to collect a royalty on books. Although Walter Crane was pleased that Caldecott got a royalty, he was also upset that he couldn't get his agreement changed so that he could also get a royalty.

At the time of the Picture Books, most toy books had blank pages on the backs of the illustrations. Evans decided to create the books with no blank pages. Other than that, Evans agreed to allow Caldecott to work in his own style after Evans taught him the process of watercolor illustration. The two men also agreed that Caldecott would select the subjects for the two picture books that would be published near Christmas each year as long as they continued to make enough money.

The three major design elements in the Picture Books are the sepia line drawings, color plates, and text type. In his Picture Books, Caldecott didn't use the heavy black borders common to illustrations at the time. He also preferred illustrations that weren't colored because the color

Caldecott brought new life to traditional rhymes and songs,
as seen in this illustration from "Hey Diddle Diddle".

pulled attention away from the lines. He did like to do covers that would catch the attention of anyone walking by a display of the books.

Unlike other picture book artists of the time, Caldecott didn't do original subjects, but selected traditional rhymes and songs. From 1878 through 1885, Caldecott spent each spring and early part of the summer selecting two subjects for the Picture Books he'd illustrate that year. Juliana Ewing, as well as other friends and fans, offered suggestions for subjects. Caldecott carefully considered each one, but always made the final decision himself.

In starting a Picture Book, Caldecott first made a dummy book. The dummy book had blank pages of the same size and number as the final book. He used this book to plan what text and illustration would appear on each page. He often made small changes in the words to so that the text would blend more easily with his illustrations.

Caldecott used pen and ink on a smooth-faced writing paper for the final copy. Someone in the publishing company photographed the drawings on wood, then Evans or one of his staff engraved them "in facsimile." If Evans engraved the pictures personally, the initials "E. E." appear in the illustrations. Otherwise, one of his employees did the engraving.

After the engraving, Evans sent the proofs to Caldecott, who critiqued the engraving and colored the pictures. He used pink, red, blue, yellow, gray, and brown ink. He made other colors by combining two or more of the primary colors—such as combining blue and yellow to make green. He outlined the pictures in brown, instead of the black ink other artists usually preferred. In the early editions, the colors glowed warmly. When the books were re-issued in later years, the colors used were brighter and somewhat harsher.

Finally the pages were printed and sewn to stiff card covers measuring nine inches wide by eight inches high. The Picture Books were ready to sell.

In the fall of 1878, George Routledge & Sons published 10,000 copies of the first two Picture Books, *The House that Jack Built* and *The Diverting History of John Gilpin*. Frederick Warne and Company later reprinted the books. The cost at the time was one shilling each (five pence in today's British currency).

William Clough, a friend and former coworker at Manchester and Salford Bank, wrote to Caldecott to praise *The House that Jack Built*. In a December 13, 1878, letter from Hotel Gray et d'Albion in Cannes, Caldecott replied, "I am flattered and pleased by your writing so swiftly to tell me that the effect of the *House that Jack Built* was upon you so marvellous. 2 or 3 notices have been read by the visitors to this hotel and I am asked if I am any relation to the gifted artist."

Caldecott included a semi-hidden "secret" in the first illustration in *The Diverting History of John Gilpin*. If the book is given a one-quarter turn, the cat near the bottom of that page becomes a self-portrait of Caldecott.

Not only friends, but reviewers liked the first two Picture Books. Nearly every reviewer gave the books a good review. A reviewer for *Punch* called *The Diverting History of John Gilpin* "*the* book for children." A reviewer in *The Times* said, "In a few strokes, dashed off apparently at random, he can portray a scene or incident to the full as correctly and completely, and far more lucidly than Mr. Crane in his later and far more elaborate style." The reviewer went on to call the illustrations "the very essence of all illustration for children's books."

A reviewer in the December 19, 1878, issue of *The Nation* said, "Mr. R. Caldecott's latest caricatures should not be overlooked by purveyors for the nursery. His "John Gilpin" and "The House that Jack Built" (Routledge) are *sui generis*, and irresistibly funny as well as clever. One hardly knows which to admire most—the full page color-prints, or the outline sketches in the brown ink of the text. Happy the generation that is brought up on such masters as Mr. Caldecott and Mr. Crane."

The first printing of the first two Picture Books sold out before a second printing could be ordered. An additional 40,000 copies sold within a few months. Six months after the first two Picture Books were released, Caldecott received £375 royalty.

Caldecott once asked for a higher royalty, but Evans said that the price of the books needed to be kept low or the sales would suffer. Caldecott reluctantly agreed to keep his royalty as it was. He often commented on his low pay. He once said, "I get a small royalty—a small, small royalty."

Caldecott thought publishers profited too much from books, while artists and authors were paid too little. He once drew a sketch titled "The Profits of a Book." The sketch showed a rich publisher with a bag of gold and the author, artist, and engraver with their tiny shares. Evans refused to publish the drawing in *A Sketch-Book of R. Caldecott's*. Even with their differences, Evans once said of Caldecott, "He is, by far, the most rewarding artist I have ever worked with."

In a December 16, 1883, letter to Juliana Ewing, Caldecott said, "I could not afford to do the *Picture Books* if the circulation were to fall much—and I am quite prepared for this event because of the ever-increasing competition of the many lovely and imaginative publications which are spread about in window and stall." Luckily the books continued to sell well.

His royalty increased to a penny farthing (6¼%) in 1881 and to three half-pence (12½%) in 1883. The Picture Books did provide a nice income for Caldecott and the publisher as well. In a March 4, 1883, letter to Juliana Ewing, he said, "Picture Books—on which I depend for some necessary luxuries of life. . . ."

In the spring of 1879, Caldecott wrote to a friend saying he had completed the dummy for either *Elegy on the Death of a Mad Dog* or *The Babes in the Wood* (which one is unclear) on a train between Florence and Bologna.

Elegy on the Death of a Mad Dog was the subject of a parody during World War I. The parody's illustrations, based on Caldecott's original illustrations, showed the head of the Kaiser of Germany in place of the mad dog's head.

In *The Babes in the Wood*, Caldecott drew himself as the character described as "A gentleman of good account . . . sore sicke he was, and like to dye, ..." The illustration showed Caldecott's awareness of his own ill health. A reviewer in *The Nation* accused Caldecott of poor taste in treating a sad situation with humor.

Caldecott didn't use only himself in his illustrations. Caldecott used Evans as the basis for one of the "ruffians strong" in *The Babes in the Wood*.

Caldecott also didn't let the sketches of the places he'd been go to waste. English poet Austin Dobson said, "The open-air life of England, with all its freshness and breeziness, its pastoral seduction and its picturesque environment, is everywhere present in his work."

Much of the area around Whitchurch Caldecott had previously sketched appeared in the Picture Books. For

Caldecott made his books realistic by using scenes taken from his life, as in the main street shown in *The Great Panjandrum himself.*

example, the Malpas Church tower is in *The Babes in the Wood, Bye, Baby Bunting,* and *The Fox Jumps over the Parson's Gate.* The main street of Whitchurch appears in *The Great Panjandrum himself.* Brook House Farm at Hanmer near Whitchurch became the model for *The House that Jack Built.*

Whitchurch wasn't the only area Caldecott used for his illustrations. Several scenes around Chelsfield including the school, the Court Lodge, and the church where Caldecott was married were featured in *The Three Jovial Huntsmen.*

R. Caldecott's Picture Book: Volume 1 was published

in 1879. The book includes the first four Picture Books: *The Diverting History of John Gilpin*, *The House that Jack Built*, *The Babes in the Wood*, and *Elegy on the Death of a Mad Dog*.

After that book was published, Caldecott received a fan letter from Robert Drane, a pharmacist who was an avid bird enthusiast and collector. Caldecott's answer in a June 22, 1880, letter showed he didn't take himself too seriously. He said, in part, "Your note of 22 May is very complimentary to me—in it you tell me you are going to *preserve* for future generations a copy of my volume of *Picture Books*. I am very glad. I hope others will do the same, and that future generations will feel blessed, be content, and not knock the nose off my statue."

In the early 1880s, Caldecott illustrated books by Edwin Waugh, including a version of the rhyme "Old Cronies" as *The Three Jolly Hunters*. Caldecott made a few changes to the words and wrote another verse. The book became the Picture Book *The Three Jovial Huntsmen*, published in 1880. Caldecott didn't give Waugh credit in the book, which was unlike him. Caldecott said he thought everyone knew the story. He used much of another old Lancashire dialect version of they rhyme that had been around for several hundred years.

Rupert Potter, the father of author and illustrator Beatrix Potter, bought the complete set of sketches to *The Three Jovial Huntsmen* for £80. Although Caldecott rarely allowed the illustrations from the Picture Books to be sold separately, Mr. Potter also bought two small pen and ink sketches from *Sing a Song for Sixpence* and/or *A Frog he would a-wooing go*. Potter wanted his daughter to study the drawings for her own work. She learned to draw partly by copying the illustrations. In 1896, she tried to duplicate the style of the drawings, but gave up in frustration.

Beatrix Potter later said, "We bought his picture books eagerly as they came out. I have the greatest admiration for his work—a jealous appreciation; for I think that others, whose names are commonly bracketed with his, are not on the same plane at all as artist-illustrators."

The original rhyme for the Picture Book *Sing a Song for Sixpence*, published in 1880, was "Sing a Song of Sixpence." The original rhyme first appeared in 1820. The rhyme was based on the "Cato Street Conspiracy" in which 24 men planned to murder the entire government Cabinet. When their plan was discovered, the potential murderers quickly started to tattle ("sing") on the others, in the hope of saving themselves.

Caldecott changed the word "of" to "for" in the title of his book to create a more complex story. The model for the young Queen in the book was the granddaughter of A. J. Mundella, who bought Caldecott's painting *The Three Huntsmen*, which was on exhibit at the Royal Academy in 1878.

Juliana Ewing praised *The Three Jovial Huntsmen* and *Sing a Song for Sixpence* highly. Caldecott answered her in a November 25, 1880, letter saying, "It is very pleasant to me—to us—to have your good opinion of these last books. You are 1 at whom I feel that I specially aim when I am making the drawings."

Caldecott didn't always find selecting the subjects for Picture Books easy. In a November 24, 1880, letter to

The young queen has tea in Caldecott's illustration
for *Sing a Song for Sixpence*.

friend Frederick Locker-Lampson, Caldecott said, "Evans wishes me to do 2 more on same items to complete another volume of 4. I have not yet found 2 new subjects. *I want them.*"

Caldecott did find his two new subjects. *The Queen of Hearts* and *The Farmer's Boy* were published in 1881. The Caroline Miller Parker Collection at the Houghton Library of the Harvard College Library has *The Queen of Hearts* bound in red morocco leather with intricate tooling and a queen of hearts playing card set in the cover. Caldecott considered expanding *The Queen of Hearts* at some point in the future, but he didn't live long enough to do the project.

R. Caldecott's Picture Book: Volume 2 was also published in 1881. The book contained *The Three Jovial Huntsmen*, *Sing a Song for Sixpence*, *The Queen of Hearts*, and *The Farmer's Boy*. That same year, all eight of the Picture Books were published in one volume titled *R. Caldecott's Collection of Pictures and Songs*.

Soon after *The Milkmaid; Hey Diddle Diddle* was published in 1882, violin collector W. Heron Allen wrote to Caldecott to praise him for his illustration of the violin. Heron said the violin's proportions and details were "scientifically correct" even if they were in a "frivolous picture."

Heron asked Caldecott's permission to reproduce the cat and the fiddle from the front cover on the back of the title page of his own book because "the representation ought to be perpetuated as something more than the title cover of a picture book." No one knows if the permission was granted, but Caldecott valued the praise. He said to Frederick Locker-Lampson, "The above is a kind of compliment which I really appreciate, because it evidently comes from a severe sort of man."

When illustrator Kate Greenaway saw Caldecott's illustrations for *Hey Diddle Diddle*, she wrote to Frederick Locker-Lampson and said, "They are uncommonly clever. The Dish running away with the spoon—you can't imagine how much he has made of it. I wish I had such a mind. I'm feeling very low about my own powers just now."

Caldecott started to become bored with the work on the series of Picture Books. He devised ways to perk up his interest. In *Bye, Baby Bunting*, published in 1882, he used illustrations from other Picture Books as wall decorations in the new illustrations.

One of the illustrations in *A Frog he would a wooing go*, published in 1883, features a peacock feather, the emblem of the Aesthetic Movement, above a fireplace mantle. Some people say he used the feather to show his support of the Movement's goal, which was to encourage appreciation of the arts.

Many critics consider *A Frog he would a wooing go* to be some of Caldecott's best work. At least one critic disagreed. A review in the December 13, 1883, issue of *The Nation* said the illustrations were "below his average" and "unworthy of the series."

The unflattering review didn't hurt the sales of Caldecott's books. The Picture Books continued to be successful. Each new title added to the popularity of previous titles. Most titles of the series sold between 6,000 and 7,000 copies a year. Sales of Caldecott's Picture Books

When Caldecott became bored with his picture books, he added elements into the drawings, such as this feather from the Aesthetic Movement in an illustration from *A Frog he would a-wooing go.*

reached 867,000 copies by early 1884. Notes kept by Caldecott's brother Alfred say that *The Diverting History of John Gilpin* alone sold about 112,000 copies in the first ten years.

The Hey Diddle Diddle Picture Book, published in 1883, contained *The Milkmaid; Hey Diddle Diddle, Bye Baby Bunting, A Frog he would a-wooing go,* and *The Fox Jumps over the Parson's Gate.*

Caldecott's lack of enthusiasm for the series of Picture Books continued. On November 5, 1884, he wrote to Evans and said, "As to future *Picture Books* I do not want to do any more of this kind: but I shall be glad to hear if you and Routledges have a strong opinion that a couple more should be done." Obviously Evans and the publisher wanted more Picture Books. The following year, Caldecott illustrated the last two of his Picture Books: *Mrs. Mary Blaize: An Elegy on the Glory of her Sex* and *The Great Panjandrum himself.*

In January 1885, a few weeks after *Come Lasses and Lads* was published, many of Caldecott's friends and business associates gathered in a place on Victoria Street, Westminster. The "lasses and lads" from the Picture Book danced to a fiddler playing an old English tune. The fiddler wasn't completely familiar with the tune and "played it wrong."

While working on *The Great Panjandrum himself,* published in 1885, Caldecott wrote, "I have made one suggestion—change 'grand' for 'great' in panjandrum. Think it most likely that it should be 'grand': but I happen to have gone by the 1st reading sent me and I have called him the *Great* on the cover &c. so we had better be consistent all through."

Although not specifically mentioned in *Mrs. Mary Blaize: An Elegy on the Glory of her Sex,* published in 1885, the main character is a pawn broker. Caldecott used the pawn broker symbol of three balls in the illustration and a line of text reads, "She freely let to all the poor who left a pledge behind." The illustration of the record book Mrs. Mary Blaize uses to keep track of the transactions hangs on the counter. Caldecott put his initials in the record book.

Because Caldecott had left on his trip to the United States before his last two Picture Books were published, he never saw the final copies of *Mrs. Mary Blaize* and *The Great Panjandrum himself.*

The Panjandrum Picture Book was published in 1885. The book contained *Come Lasses and Lads, Ride a Cock Horse to Banbury Cross; A Farmer went trotting upon his Gray Mare*; *Mrs. Mary Blaize: An Elegy on the Glory of her Sex;* and *The Great Panjandrum himself.*

R. Caldecott's Second Collection of Pictures and Songs was also published in 1885. The book contained both *The Hey Diddle Diddle Picture Book* and *The Panjandrum Picture Book*, which meant that second eight of Caldecott's Picture Books became available in one volume.

The popularity of the Picture Books couldn't be denied. Five months after his death in 1886, over 800,000 copies of Caldecott's Picture Books had been sold.

In 1887, Routledge released an "edition de luxe" of the Picture Books. The publisher and Edmund Evans autographed each of the 1,000 copies of the limited edition of all sixteen Picture Books in one volume titled *The Complete Collection of Randolph Caldecott's Pictures and Songs*. The edition, printed on larger paper, sold out immediately. Evans said, "I wished I had printed three or four thousand instead of one thousand."

Miniature Picture Books, a much smaller size of the Picture Books, were published in 1906 and 1907. The individual Picture Books and four volumes of four books each were issued.

By the end of 1888, ten years after the first Picture Book was released, Caldecott's royalties reached about £3,400. That showed how much children loved the Pic-

Caldecott's work, such as this illustration from *The Milkmaid; Hey Diddle Diddle,* touched many lives over the years.

ture Books. The lively characters were in complete contrast to Caldecott's poor health and often serious, quiet manner. Maurice Sendak, who won the Caldecott Medal for *Where the Wild Things Are*, said, "I can't think of Caldecott without thinking of music and dance," and "No one in a Caldecott book ever stands still. If the characters are not dancing, they are itching to dance. They never walk; they skip."

Frederic Melcher, who established the Caldecott Award, summed up Caldecott's influence when he said, "His picture books have been the happy companions of succeeding generations of children, and the spirit of his work has inspired to excellence the artists who today enchant our children."

Chapter Nine

The Final Months

A FEW MONTHS after his 39th birthday, Randolph Caldecott really began to slow down and started feeling older. In his usual style, he joked about it in a July 18, 1885, letter to friend Frederick Locker-Lampson. Caldecott said, "P.S. I am beginning to feel old—it is through discovering once or twice lately that I have not been the youngest man in the company."

Later that year, the Caldecotts sold their lease at 24 Holland Street in Kensington to prepare for a trip to the United States on a tour similar to that of the Harz Mountains trip. Caldecott promised the London *Graphic* a series of sketches about American life. Caldecott enjoyed the idea of a sketching tour and thought the change in climate could help his health.

On October 18, 1885, Caldecott wrote to Locker-Lampson saying, "It was the suggestion of you and Mrs Locker—you will remember—that we should go to America. We shall sail by Cunard ship 'Aurania' on 31st inst. I propose to take an easy tour—be guided by circumstances, of which the climate may be the chief. It may be pleasant to go quietly down the Eastern States to Florida and eventually on through New Orleans to South

California, then up to North California and through Colorado and home by Boston?"

Caldecott was hoping the food would be good. In the same letter to Locker-Lampson, he said, "At present I am hoping that my experience on the vessel may not cause me to call a man—when I am very angry in the future—'the son of a sea-cook'—a time-honoured, but somewhat disused, epithet."

The trip across the ocean took twelve days, a day longer than usual, thanks to the storms. Caldecott described the journey in a November 18, 1885, letter to Locker-Lampson in which he said, " . . . we have not suffered shipwreck, altho' we had not an agreeable passage altogether." He went on to say, "Mrs. C was not very well. I was not sea-sick at all; but was a little light-headed and lost some rest. I felt the confinement of the cabin for a day or two, and hated the plunging of the remorseless, resistless vessel. There was no getting off." Again, his good humor was evident when he wrote, "We hope there will be an overland route discovered by the time of our return."

Caldecott spent much of his time on the ship sketching the passengers, the cabins, and the crew. A small boy travelling by himself while making "The Grand Tour of Europe" appears in many of the sketches. While on the ship, Caldecott also spent a great deal of time resting, but never felt rested.

A representative of the New York *Daily Graphic* met the Caldecotts in New York. While taking the visitors to their hotel, he tried to talk them into staying in New York a few days. Caldecott declined, saying he wanted

Although suffering from ill health, Caldecott spent time on the ship sketching passengers and scenes around him.

to get to a warmer climate as soon as possible.

The following morning the Caldecotts stepped aboard a train going south. Caldecott didn't like the large number of billboards he could see from his train window. He made a sketch of horses using the billboards as hurdles in a hunting scene.

The Caldecotts first stopped in Philadelphia. The

horse railways running along the main streets of Philadelphia made both of them nervous. Caldecott liked the clean streets and red houses with white doors. At the same time, he "was shocked by the lavish display of shop-signs and other street advertisements, and bewildered by the cobweb of telegraph wires and the forests of poles in the chief streets." As soon as Caldecott had made a few sketches, the couple left for Washington, D.C.

Congress wasn't in session when the Caldecotts arrived in Washington, D.C. Caldecott said, "The Capitol at Washington was dull during my visit. There were no statesmen or lobbyists, only a few country people looking at the Chambers, and at the historical pictures in the Rotunda." He described the area by saying, "Washington is a fine town with imposing public buildings and wide, clean streets."

By then, Caldecott started becoming noticeably more ill and exhausted each day. Marian Caldecott wanted to skip the next scheduled stop in Charleston, South Carolina. Caldecott insisted they stop just long enough for him to do a few sketches. He titled the last sketch he ever did "Negroes Loading Cotton Bales in Charleston." Caldecott was able to complete only nine drawings during the entire United States trip.

Finally, in early December, the Caldecotts settled into the Magnolia Hotel in St. Augustine, Florida, to wait out the winter.

Unfortunately, that year Florida went through its coldest winter in 50 years. The warm weather Caldecott needed for his health didn't arrive. Marian wrote to Jane

"Negroes Loading Cotton Bales in Charleston,"
Caldecott's last completed drawing.

Locker-Lampson with the news that the weakness in Caldecott's heart complicated his "severe attack of gastritis."

By the end of January, Caldecott started eating better and gaining strength. But, on a Saturday less than three weeks later, Marian summoned a doctor. Nothing more could be done. Randolph Caldecott soon died.

Dr. H. Caruthers wrote on the death certificate, "This certifies that Mr. Randolph Caldecott, age 39, Born in Chester Engd. died at St Augustine, Fla. February 13, 1886, of organic disease of the heart."

Caldecott was buried in Evergreen Cemetery in St. Augustine. At the time, the cemetery held only about 20 graves. The error in date on the tombstone (the 12th instead of the 13th) would likely have bothered someone like Caldecott who was a perfectionist. The Randolph Caldecott Society of America now tends the grave. The grave site is near lot #31 and enclosed by a concrete railing with four standing corner posts.

When Caldecott's long-time friend and business associate Thomas Armstrong learned of Caldecott's death, he telegraphed Marian and asked if she needed someone else with her during "this difficult time." She telegraphed back a simple reply: "No."

Caldecott's death affected not only his family and friends, but business associates and fans as well. Kate Greenaway said, "Isn't it sad about Mr. Caldecott? The last I heard he was so much better—and now—dead. It looks quite horrid to see the black-bordered card with his books in the shop windows—it feels horrid to want to sell his books, somehow, just yet."

A. J. Mundella, the member of Parliament who bought Caldecott's painting *The Three Huntsmen*, said simply, "He is indeed a national loss."

Randolph Caldecott would be missed by many, not only for his art ability, but also for the man he was. Frederick Locker-Lampson said, "Poor Caldecott! His friends were much attached to him. He had feeling and ideas, and manners, which made him welcome in any society; but alas, all was trammeled, not obscured, by deplorably bad health."

After Caldecott's death, Marian moved to Tunbridge Wells, Kent. She continued to see various works of Caldecott published and exhibited, and often took part in the processes.

Two years after his death, some of Caldecott's friends and fellow artists arranged· an exhibition of his work. They chose the Brasenose Club in Manchester as the exhibition site. Marian Caldecott thought the idea was wonderful and loaned them many pieces from her private collection for the event.

In 1888, George Routledge and Sons published *The Complete Collection of Randolph Caldecott's Contributions to the "Graphic."* The book, published in a limited edition of 1,250 numbered copies, is a collection of Caldecott's illustrations that appeared in the *Graphic* between 1876 and 1886. That means the "complete" in the book's title inaccurate because Caldecott's contributions to the magazine from 1872 and 1874 aren't included.

Marian Caldecott wasn't pleased with the 1899 publication of *Lightning Sketches for "The House that Jack Built."* She thought Caldecott's quick sketches in planning the book looked too hurried and feared his reputation would be harmed.

Marian Caldecott died on June 12, 1932, after being a widow for more years than her husband was alive. She is buried with her sister Amy Alice Brind in Tunbridge Wells.

The value of the Caldecott estate was nearly £14,000 (about $22,500), a large amount for the time. She bequeathed most of Caldecott's art to Randolph's brother Alfred Caldecott, Randolph's nephew Clement Caldecott, and Marian's nephew John Randolph Anthony. Although Randolph Caldecott died in 1886, his characters still live in books and museums.

Chapter Ten

Randolph Caldecott Remembered

AFTER RANDOLPH CALDECOTT'S death in 1886, several of his friends formed a committee. They hired Sir Alfred Gilbert to design a memorial to Caldecott. The tablet depicts a child similar to those Caldecott illustrated in *Breton Folk*. The child is holding a medallion with a bas-relief likeness of Caldecott. An inscription reads, "An artist whose sweet and dainty grace has not been in its kind surpassed: whose humour was as quaint as it was inexhaustible."

The memorial tablet was placed in the artist's corner, the far right-hand corner of the OBE Chapel, of the crypt of St. Paul's Cathedral in London. Plaques were also placed at Caldecott's birthplace at 15 Bridge Street in Chester, in the North-West Apse of Chester Cathedral, and 46 Great Russell Street in London.

The February 27, 1886, issue of *Punch* honored Caldecott with the following poem:

> *All that flow of fun, and all*
> *That fount of charm found in his fancy,*
> *Are stopped! Yet will he hold us all thrall*
> *By his fine art's sweet necromancy,*

> *Children and seniors many a year;*
> *For long 'twill be ere a new-comer,*
> *Fireside or nursery holdeth dear*
> *As him whose life ceased in its summer.*

Although Henry Blackburn knew Caldecott disliked publicity and valued his privacy, he wrote *Randolph Caldecott: A Personal Memoir of His Early Art Career*, published by Sampson, Low, Marston Searle & Rivington in 1887.

A review of Blackburn's memoir in the *New York Art Amateur* read, "The name of Caldecott and the charming visions it evokes are still fresh in the minds of young and old, and the shock of his untimely death seems but of yesterday. We must be grateful for any 'touch of the vanished hand' and any glimpse, however slight, of so genial and gifted a personality."

After Marian Caldecott died in 1932, seven of Caldecott's sketchbooks and 259 pictures became a part of the collection at the Victoria and Albert Museum. The British Museum in London has 119 drawings that aren't on view, but can be examined in the Students' Room. Some of the other museums that have Caldecott's works include a self-portrait at the Aberdeen City Art Gallery and Museums (Aberdeen, Scotland), one or more illustrations from *The Diverting History of John Gilpin* at the Birmingham City Museum and Art Gallery (Birmingham, West Midlands, England), City Art Gallery (Manchester, England), Heritage Centre (Whitchurch, Shropshire, England), several books in the Colin Mears Collection at the Museum and Art Gallery

$5.00

January / February 1986

The Horn Book

Magazine

ABOUT BOOKS FOR CHILDREN AND YOUNG ADULTS

(Worthing, West Sussex, England), Whitworth Art Gallery (Manchester, England), and many works available by special arrangement at the Worcester City Museum and Art Gallery (Worcester, Surrey, England). The Caroline Miller Parker Collection at the Houghton Library of the Harvard College Library in Cambridge, Massachusetts, also contains many of Caldecott's works.

In the United States, Caldecott was given the honor of having his drawing of the three jovial huntsmen as part of the front cover of *The Horn Book Magazine* for 59 of the first 61 years of the magazine's existence.

The covers of the November/December 1985 through September/October 1986 issues of *The Horn Book Magazine* feature a homage to Caldecott by Maurice Sendak, a Caldecott Medal winner. The illustration features Caldecott with the cat and the fiddle, a girl, a dog, and one of Sendak's own "Wild Things" (characters in his Caldecott-winning book) watching the artist draw. The illustration is based on a drawing Caldecott made called "Sketching under Difficulties" that he drew while working on *Breton Folk*.

The Caldecott Foundation

In the late 1800s, Leila Rendel established a refuge for homeless and unwanted children in the East End of London. At the time, the organization was called St Pancras Day Nursery.

Rendel decorated the walls of the bedroom with illustrations from Randolph Caldecott's Picture Books. In 1911, the organization formally became known as "The Caldecott Community." The home eventually moved to

Mersham-le-Hatch in Kent, the country home of the Knatchbull family. The name of the organization was changed to "The Caldecott Foundation."

The primary purpose of The Caldecott Foundation charitable organization is "to create a therapeutic ambiance where a child and young person can grow in every sense of the word; physically, socially, emotionally and intellectually. Beginning to repair some of the damage to his or her inner world quite often brought about by traumatic and disrupted early events & difficulties."

More information about The Caldecott Foundation can be found at the following web site: www.caldecottfoundation.org.

The Caldecott Medal

The Children's Librarians' Section of the American Library Association (ALA) established the Caldecott Medal as a companion to the Newbery Medal. The awards recognize "the most distinguished contribution to American literature for children," the Newbery for text and the Caldecott for illustration. In 1938, ALA presented the first Caldecott Medal to Dorothy Lathrop, illustrator of *Animals of the Bible*, with text selected by Helen Dean Fish, and published by Lippincott.

René Paul Chambellan designed the Caldecott Medal. He studied a collection of Caldecott's works before beginning his own design. The front of the medal pictures John Gilpin's ride with the words "THE CALDECOTT MEDAL" circling the figure. The back of the medal pictures a pie containing four-and-twenty blackbirds to be set before the king. The words "For the most distinguished American picture book for children" circle the top in two lines. The words "Awarded annually by the children's and school librarians sections of the American Library Association" circle the bottom in four lines.

Until the early 1960s the award was known as "The Randolph J. Caldecott Medal." Finally someone pointed out that Caldecott had no middle initial. The "J." disappeared from the award's name.

Committees of fourteen members and one chairperson select the Caldecott Award each year. All members of the committee must be members of the ALA's Association for Library Service to Children. After contacting each other throughout the year to discuss books for consideration, the committee makes its final decision during the ALA mid-winter conference, usually held in late January or early February. The committee selects the book whose illustrator will receive the bronze, or top, award. The committee also recognizes one or more "Honor Books," formerly known as "Runners-up." Illustrators of the Honor Books receive a silver medal.

The actual process of selecting the award changes with each committee, but all have to follow the same basic rules. Some primary qualifications for a book to be considered for the Caldecott Medal are:

* The illustrator must be a citizen or resident of the United States.
* The book must be a "picture book for children."
* The book must be "distinguished" in comparison to other books.

* The illustrations must be original; they cannot be reprinted or compiled from other sources.
* The book must be published in the United States during the preceding year. For example, only books originally published in 1937 were eligible for the first award in 1938.
* Only an individual book, not the artist's other works, should be considered in the selection of the winner.

The Caldecott winners are announced soon after the committee makes its final decision. Illustrators of the Caldecott Medal books usually attend the ALA summer conference. A special ceremony honors the illustrators. During the ceremony, the illustrator makes a speech and receives the actual Caldecott Medal.

In her Caldecott Medal acceptance speech for *Cinderella* (Scribner) in 1955, Marcia Brown said, "An artist cannot help feeling deeply honored to receive an award bearing the name of Randolph Caldecott, one of the happiest spirits in children's books."

Peter Spier told of an early experience he had with Caldecott's Picture Books during his Caldecott Medal acceptance speech for *Noah's Ark* (Doubleday) in 1978. His father owned a collection of Caldecott's books, most of them first editions. When Spier was about three years old, he used a red crayon to scribble on every page of one of the books. He said, "I do not recall the spanking I was given, although my father assures me that it was fairly meted out." When Spier told his father that *Noah's Ark* had won the Caldecott Medal, his father gave him the entire collection of Caldecott's books.

Richard Egielski, in his Caldecott Medal acceptance speech for *Hey, Al!*, written by Arthur Yorinks, (Farrar) in 1987, said, "I feel honored not just because of the prestige and praise that come with this award, but also because now my name will always be linked with Randolph Caldecott."

Maurice Sendak, creator of the 1964 Caldecott Medal book *Where the Wild Things Are* (Harper), is an avid Randolph Caldecott fan. He said, "Caldecott is an illustrator, a songwriter, a choreographer, a stage manager—he is, simply, superb. He can take four lines of verse with little meaning in themselves and stretch them into a book with tremendous meaning—not overloaded, no sentimentality in it."

Trina Schart Hyman won the 1985 Caldecott Medal for *Saint George and the Dragon*, written by Margaret Hodges (Little, Brown). She included the phrase "Apologies to R.C." in an illustration for *On to Wildcombe Fair*, by Patricia Lee Gauch (Kingswood, the World's Work, 1979), because the illustration was in a similar style to that of Randolph Caldecott.

The Caldecott Medal has become one of the most important awards in children's, as well as adult, literature. Thanks to the award, recognition of the importance of children's books, and illustrations in particular, has increased greatly. The Caldecott Medal also assures the name of Randolph Caldecott will be remembered and honored as long as the award is presented.

For more information about the Caldecott Medal, see the web site at http://www.ala.org/alsc/caldecott.html.

Illustration from *A Frog he would a-wooing go.*

The Randolph Caldecott Society UK

Journalist Kenn Oultram attended an exhibition of Randolph Caldecott's work at Manchester Library in 1973. Oultram was so impressed that he formed a Society to inspire interest in Caldecott. Ten years later, on June 18, 1983, the Society held its first formal meeting.

The mission of the Randolph Caldecott Society UK is "To promote and encourage, for the public benefit, the study and appreciation of the work and life of the artist and illustrator Randolph Caldecott (1846-1886)."

Since the inauguration in 1983, at least two meetings have been held each year. One meeting is a visit to an area somehow related to Caldecott or his work. The other meeting is held on March 22, the anniversary of Caldecott's birth. At the latter meeting, flowers are laid at the memorial in Chester Cathedral.

Some of the activities of the Randolph Caldecott Society include organizing visits to areas where Caldecott lived or sketched, providing funds for art students, offering guest lectures, commemorating Caldecott's birth, and hosting members of the Randolph Caldecott Society of America when visiting England.

The Randolph Caldecott Society UK web site at www.randolphcaldecott.org.uk provides a wealth of information about Caldecott, including text and illustrations from many of his works.

The Randolph Caldecott Society of America

Gwen Reichert and her father discovered Caldecott's grave site in St. Augustine, Florida, had been neglected and had the site restored. In 1967, Reichert and her husband, Allan, served as "lay caretakers" of the grave until the Randolph Caldecott Society of America assumed the responsibility.

The Reicherts, along with several other people, founded the Randolph Caldecott Society of America in 1983. The organization holds annual meetings in March, the month of Caldecott's birth.

The purposes of the Randolph Caldecott Society of America are:

* To bring together those people who are dedicated to the remembrance, appreciation, and promotion of English Illustrator, Painter and Sculptor, Randolph Caldecott (1846-1886) and his art.
* To serve as a lay caretaker of Caldecott's grave in Evergreen Cemetery, St. Augustine, Florida.
* To maintain a floral tribute on the grave.
* To mail out a membership packet of informative

materials to all new members.
* To hold an annual General Meeting for the bene-
fit of members.
* To donate the annual Caldecott Medal-winning
book, along with the winning Honor Book(s), to
the local Public Library's "Randolph Caldecott
Children's Room."
* To maintain a Caldecott Society sign on the St.
Augustine Community Organizations Display
Board(s).
* To produce and distribute a brochure and to
maintain a web site about Caldecott.
* To contribute to the annual student Art Award.
* To give presentations on the life and art of Calde-
cott upon request.
* To award and Honorary Membership to a person
who has exhibited outstanding support of the So-
ciety as determined by the membership of the
Society, and who promotes and/or collects the
work of Caldecott.
* To support other projects deemed appropriate by
the Society.

At this writing, membership fees in the Randolph
Caldecott Society of America are easily affordable, especially considering the materials, including two books,
that are part of the membership packet.

For more information about the Randolph Caldecott
Society of America, see the web site www.rcsa.com or
contact Gwen P. Reichert, president, 112 Crooked Tree
Trail, St. Augustine, FL 32086.

A Caldecott book plate,
filled with his trademark detail.

Randolph Caldecott

Purchasing Works of Randolph Caldecott

Although many of Randolph Caldecott's fine art pieces are in museums, original paintings and other works occasionally become available for sale. The value of the works vary from several hundred to several thousand dollars. The size, medium, subject, and condition are all factors in determining the price.

On rare occasions, one of Caldecott's letters becomes available. One of his letters containing a sketch will sell for about £100-150 (about $150-250 U.S.).

Some dealers cut out pages of Caldecott's books, particularly from the Picture Books and other books with color illustrations, and mount the individual pictures to be sold as wall hangings. A set of about six mounted pictures sells for about £125-150 (about $200-250 U.S.). Occasionally, a single mounted illustration from the Picture Books can be found for a few pounds.

All of Randolph Caldecott's books are out-of-print at this writing, but used editions, particularly reprints, can be found at specialty used books stores relatively frequently. Some original editions of Caldecott's Picture Books and other volumes in which many copies were printed have been sold for £200 or more (about $325 U.S.). Copies of some of the limited editions of books, such as *The Complete Collection of Randolph Caldecott's Contributions to the "Graphic"*, have sold for over £750 (about $1,200 U.S.).

Only 1,250 copies of *The Complete Collection of Randolph Caldecott's Contribution to the "Graphic"* were printed. The preface contains a memorial poem by "H. E. D." The poem captures much of Caldecott's lasting influence in a few lines. The poem reads

Alas poor Caldecott! We hoped in vain
We should not lose thy presence yet awhile.
Thou hadst no rival in thine own quaint style;
Vacant thy place may evermore remain.
Thy pencil drew, with loving, faithful care,
Each phase of human nature in its turn.
So that one looked and laughed, but yet could learn
To love all men the more for what was there.
Old folks would smile, and seem to see once more
The men and manners of a day gone by,
Whilst infants o'er thy "Picture Books" would pore,
And feast on Dreamland scenes with wondering eye.

Timeline of Major Events
Surrounding Randolph Caldecott

1846   Randolph Caldecott was born at 150 Bridge Street in Chester, Cheshire, England, on March 22.

1848   The Caldecott family moved to Crook Street.

1852   Randolph Caldecott and his mother became ill with rheumatic fever in August. Mary Dinah Brookes Caldecott died on August 21.

1852   Caldecott began his education at the King's School.

1860   The Caldecott family moved to Boughton.

1861   Caldecott moved to Whitchurch and started working as a clerk at the Whitchurch and Ellesmere Bank.

1861   Caldecott's first published illustration (the Queen Hotel fire) appeared in the *Illustrated London News* on December 7.

1867   Caldecott moved to Manchester to work at the Manchester and Salford Bank.

1868   Caldecott's first drawings in *Will o' the Wisp*

were published in the July issue.

1869   Caldecott's first artwork was exhibited at the Royal Manchester Institution.

1870   Caldecott met Thomas Armstrong in May.

1871   Caldecott's first illustrations in *London Society*, edited by Henry Blackburn, appeared in Volume XX.

1872   Caldecott moved to London to pursue his art full time.

1872   Caldecott's first illustration in *Punch* appeared in the June 22 issue.

1872   Caldecott's first illustration in *Graphic* appeared in the autumn issue.

1872   Caldecott worked on the illustrations for his first book, *The Harz Mountains: A Tour in the Toy Country*, written by Henry Blackburn.

1872   Caldecott was elected to the Royal Institute of Watercolour Painting.

1873   Caldecott's first illustrations published in the June issue of *Harper's New Monthly Journal*.

1873   *The Harz Mountains*, written by Henry Blackburn and with some illustrations by Caldecott, was published.

1875   *Old Christmas*, written by Washington Irving and illustrated by Caldecott, was published.

1876   Caldecott exhibited the oil painting *There*

> *were Three Ravens Sat on a Tree* and the bas-relief *Horse Fair in Brittany* at the Royal Academy.

1877   Caldecott moved to the French Riviera for health reasons. He continued to work on illustrations that appeared in the London *Graphic.*

1877   *Bracebridge Hall*, written by Washington Irving and illustrated by Caldecott, was published.

1878   *North Italian Folk*, written by Mrs. Comyns Carr and illustrated by Caldecott, was published.

1878   Caldecott met Edmund Evans and agreed to do the Picture Books. *The House that Jack Built* and *The Diverting History of John Gilpin* were published.

1879   Caldecott moved to Wybournes.

1880   Caldecott married Marian Harriet Brind on March 18.

1880   *Breton Folk*, written by Henry Blackburn and illustrated by Caldecott, was published.

1880   Caldecott became a member of the Manchester Academy of Fine Arts.

1882   The Caldecotts left Wybournes and moved to 24 Holland Street, Kensington, in June.

1882   The Caldecotts took a 21-year lease on

Broomfield, a country home in Frensham, Farnham, Surrey.

1883   *Some of Aesop's Fables with Modern Instances*, written by Alfred Caldecott and illustrated by Randolph Caldecott, was published.

1883   *Jackanapes*, written by Juliana Horatia Ewing and illustrated by Caldecott, was published.

1885   The Caldecotts left England for a sketching tour of America in October.

1885   Caldecott's last two Picture Books, *Mrs. Mary Blaize* and *The Great Panjandrum himself*, were published.

1886   Caldecott died in St. Augustine, Florida, on February 13.

1886   *Jack and the Beanstalk*, written by Hallam Tennyson and with unfinished illustrations by Caldecott, was published.

1899   Caldecott's *Lightning Sketches for "The House that Jack Built"* was published.

1900?   Wybournes burned down.

1911   The Randolph Caldecott Foundation was formally established

1932   Marian Caldecott died on June 12.

1938   The first Caldecott Medal was awarded to *Animals of the Bible*, illustrated by Dorothy P.

Lathrop and with text selected by Helen Dean Fish (Lippincott).

1983   The Randolph Caldecott Society UK was established.

1993   The Randolph Caldecott Society of America was founded.

Selected Works of Randolph Caldecott

(For a more complete list of Caldecott's works, see the appendix from *Randolph Caldecott: Lord of the Nursery*, by Rodney K. Engen, Bloomsbury Books, London, 1976)

The Picture Books

All engraved and printed by Edmund Evans; originally published by George Routledge & Sons, London and New York.

The Diverting History of John Gilpin, poem by William Cowper (1878)

The House that Jack Built (1878)

The Babes in the Wood (1879)

Elegy on the Death of a Mad Dog, poem by Oliver Goldsmith (1879)

The Three Jovial Huntsmen (1880)

Sing a Song for Sixpence (1880)

The Queen of Hearts (1881)

The Farmer's Boy (1881)

The Milkmaid; Hey Diddle Diddle (1882)

Bye, Baby Bunting (1882)

A Frog he would a-wooing go (1883)

The Fox Jumps over the Parson's Gate (1883)

Come Lasses and Lads; Ride a Cock Horse to Banbury Cross (1884)

A Farmer went trotting upon his Gray Mare (1884)

Mrs. Mary Blaize: An Elegy on the Glory of her Sex, by Oliver Goldsmith (1885)

The Great Panjandrum himself, story by Samuel Foote (1885)

Collections and Other Versions of the Picture Books

R. Caldecott's Picture Book: Volume 1 (reissue of *The Diverting History of John Gilpin, The House that Jack Built, The Babes in the Wood,* and *Elegy on the Death of a Mad Dog* in one volume, 1879)

R. Caldecott's Picture Book: Volume 2 (reissue of *The Three Jovial Huntsmen, Sing a Song for Sixpence, The Queen of Hearts,* and *The Farmer's Boy* in one volume, 1881)

R. Caldecott's Collection of Pictures and Songs (reissue of volumes 1 and 2 in a single volume, 1881)

The Hey Diddle Diddle Picture Book (reissue of *The Milkmaid; Hey Diddle Diddle, Bye, Baby Bunting, A Frog he would a-wooing go,* and *The Fox Jumps over the Parson's Gate* in one volume, 1883)

The Panjandrum Picture Book (reissue of *Come*

Lasses and Lads; Ride a Cock Horse to Banbury Cross, A Farmer went trotting upon his Gray Mare, Mrs. Mary Blaize: An Elegy on the Glory of her Sex, and *The Great Panjandrum himself* in one volume, 1885)

R. Caldecott's Second Collection of Pictures and Songs (reissue of *The Hey Diddle Diddle Picture Book* and *The Panjandrum Picture Book* in one volume, 1885)

The Complete Collection of Randolph Caldecott's Pictures and Songs with preface by Austin Dobson (limited edition of all 16 Picture Books in a single volume, 1887)

Jean Gilpin, l'histoire divertissante de la promenade a cheval [*The Diverting History of John Gilpin* in French] (New York: Frederick A. Stokes, 1878)

Miniature Picture Books (miniature editions of each title and four volumes of four titles each, 1906 and 1907)

Other Books

The Harz Mountains: A Tour in the Toy Country by Henry Blackburn (London: Sampson Low, Marston, Low & Searle, 1873). Caldecott provided the cover illustration and 27 of the 40 illustrations throughout the book.

Frank Mildmay or The Naval Officer by Captain Marryat, with a Memoir by Florence Marryat (London and New York: George Routledge & Sons, 1873). Caldecott provided six full-page illustrations.

Granny's Story Box by "the author of 'Our White

Violet,' 'Sunny Days,' etc." (neither the author nor Caldecott is mentioned in the credits, but "R. C." can be seen in some of the larger illustrations) (publisher unknown, 1873)

Baron Bruno or The Unbelieving Philosopher and other Fairy Stories by Louisa Morgan (London: Macmillan & Co., 1875). Caldecott provided eight illustrations.

Old Christmas: From the Sketch Book of Washington Irving (London: Macmillan & Co., 1875). Caldecott provided 120 illustrations.

Bracebridge Hall by Washington Irving (London: Macmillan & Co., 1877). Caldecott provided 116 illustrations.

North Italian Folk, Sketches of Town and Country Life by Mrs. Comyns Carr (London: Chatto and Windus, 1878). Caldecott provided 10 full-page and 18 half-page black-and-white illustrations; the 28 illustrations became hand-colored plates in another edition.

Breton Folk, An Artistic Tour in Brittany by Henry Blackburn (London: Sampson Low, Marston, Searle & Rivington, 1880). Caldecott provided 170 illustrations.

London Lyrics by Frederick Locker-Lampson (London: Chiswick Press, 1881). Caldecott provided the frontispiece in the London edition and three additional illustrations for the edition published by Private Press for the Book Fellows Club in New York in 1883.

What the Blackbird Said, A Story in Four Chirps by Mrs. Frederick Locker (London and New York: George

Routledge & Sons, 1881). Caldecott provided four illustrations.

Poems and Songs by Edwin Waugh (Manchester: John Heywood, 1883). Caldecott provided three photo-engraved illustrations.

Society Novelettes by F. C. Burnand, et. al. (London: Vizetelly & Co., 1883). Caldecott provided four illustrations to the story "Crossed in Love."

Some of Aesop's Fables with Modern Instances from new Translations by Alfred Caldecott, M. A. (London: Macmillan & Co., 1883)

A Sketch-Book of R. Caldecott's (London and New York: George Routledge & Sons, 1883)

Jackanapes by Juliana Horatia Ewing (London: Society for Promoting Christian Knowledge, 1883) Caldecott provided 17 illustrations.

Daddy Darwin's Dovecot, A Country Tale by Juliana Horatia Ewing (London: Society for Promoting Christian Knowledge, 1883). Caldecott provided 17 illustrations.

Lob Lie-by-the Fire, or The Luck of Lingborough by Juliana Horatia Ewing (London: Society for Promoting Christian Knowledge, 1885). Caldecott provided 19 illustrations.

Fables de la Fontaine, A Selection with Introduction, Notes and Vocabulary by Louis M. Moriarity (London: Macmillan & Co., 1885). Caldecott provided 12 electrotype black-and-white illustrations.

Jack and the Beanstalk, English Hexameters by Hallam Tennyson (London and New York: Macmillan &

Co., 1886). Caldecott's unfinished illustrations throughout 70 pages.

The Owls of Olynn Belfry, A Tale for Children by A. Y. D. (London: Field & Tuer—The Leadenhall Press; C. Simpkin, Marshall & Co.; Hamilton, Adams & Co., 1886). Caldecott provided 18 illustrations.

Randolph Caldecott's Painting Book (London: Society for Promoting Christian Knowledge, 1895)

Sporting Society or Sporting Chat and Sporting Memories edited by Fox Russell (London: Bellairs & Co., 1897). Caldecott provided the frontispiece for each of the two volumes, plus five illustrations for the story "Huntingcrop Hall" by Alfred E. T. Watson.

Lightning Sketches for "The House that Jack Built" introduced by Aubyn Trevor-Battye (London: The "Artist" in aid of the London Hospital, 1899). This book contained 30 of the first sketches Caldecott did for the Picture Book mentioned in the title.

Randolph Caldecott's Painting Book [First Series] (London and New York: Frederick Warne, 1902)

A Christmas Interlude (Chicago: The Cuneo Press, 1942). Caldecott provided 32 illustrations.

Collections of Illustrations from Periodicals or Other Books Previously Published

Scènes humoristiques (Paris: Librarie Hachette & Cie, 1882). Caldecott provided the frontispiece and color illustrations from English magazines.

Rambles in the Lake Country and other Travel Sketches by Edwin Waugh (Manchester: John Heywood, 1883). Caldecott provided three illustrations.

Randolph Caldecott's "Graphic" Pictures (London and New York: George Routledge & Sons, 1883). Caldecott provided illustrations throughout the 96 pages.

A Few Sketches by the Late Randolph Caldecott with Compliments (publisher unknown, 1886). Eight illustrations from *Breton Folk* were used in the book.

The Christmas Card Sketch Book (London: Marion & Co., 1886). Caldecott provided three illustrations.

Fascimilies of Original Sketches (Manchester: J. Galloway, 1887). Caldecott's work in *Will o' the Wisp* magazine was included on 16 pages.

More "Graphic" Pictures (London and New York: George Routledge & Sons, 1887). Caldecott provided illustrations throughout the 71 pages.

Randolph Caldecott's Last "Graphic" Pictures (London and New York: George Routledge & Sons, 1888). Caldecott provided illustrations throughout the 71 pages.

The Complete Collection of Randolph Caldecott's Contributions to the "Graphic" with a preface by Arthur Locker (London and New York: George Routledge & Sons, 1888). This book is a collection of the other *Graphic* illustrations books.

Gleanings from the "Graphic" by Randolph Caldecott (London and New York: George Routledge & Sons,

1888). Caldecott's illustrations appear throughout the 84 pages.

Catalogue of a Loan Collection of the Works of Randolph Caldecott at the Brasenose Club with memoir by George Evans (Manchester: John Heywood, 1888). Caldecott provided black-and-white illustrations for 24 pages.

Randolph Caldecott's Sketches with an Introduction by Henry Blackburn (London: Sampson Low, Marston & Co., 1889). This book has 94 pages of Caldecott's earlier sketches.

Artistic Travel, A Thousand Miles Towards the Sun, Artistic Travel in Normandy, Brittany, the Pyrenees, Spain and Algeria by Henry Blackburn (London: Sampson Low, Marston & Co., 1892). Caldecott provided 130 black-and-white illustrations.

The Art of Illustration by Henry Blackburn (London: W. H. Allen & Co., 1894). Caldecott provided 95 black-and-white illustrations.

Caldecott provided only the cover and/or frontispiece in at least ten more books.

Some Magazines and Newspapers Where Caldecott's Illustrations Appeared

(He was usually published in several different issues of each.)

Academy Notes, edited by Henry Blackburn

Academy Sketches, established by Henry Blackburn

Aunt Judy's Magazine, edited by Horatia Gatty

Belgravia: A London Magazine, edited by M. E. Braddon

Daily Graphic (New York)

The English Illustrated Magazine, edited by J. W. Comyns Carr

Graphic (Caldecott's illustrations appeared from 1872 to 1886)

Grosvenor Notes, edited by Henry Blackburn

Harper's New Monthly Magazine (sketches from *The Harz Mountains)*

Illustrated London News (Caldecott's first published illustration appeared on December 7, 1861; Caldecott is not known to have had another illustration published in this particular newspaper)

London Society, edited by Henry Blackburn

The Pictorial World

Punch

Routledge Christmas Number 1881

The Sphinx

Will o' The Wisp

Fine Art

at least 57 oil paintings

sculptures:

6 bas-reliefs in bronze including *Astrophel, A Boar*

Hunt, *The Diligence*, *Huntsmen and Hounds* (also a tinted version), *The Soldier's Farewell*, and *Three Jovial Huntsmen* (also a tinted plaster version)

- 2 tinted bas-reliefs including *Feeding the Calves* and *Huntsmen and Hounds* (also a bronze version)

- 1 bas-relief in metal titled *Horse Fair in Brittany*

- 1 tinted plaster bas-relief titled *Three Jovial Huntsmen* (also a bronze version)

- 1 wax, plaster, and bronze bas-relief titled *Girl Feeding Calves*, or sometimes, *Feeding Calves*

- 1 bronze group of three figures titled *Gossip at the Well*

- 1 frieze titled *Hunting Scene*

- 1 terra-cotta frieze titled *Horse Fair, Le Folquet, Brittany*

- 1 plaster frieze titled *The Chase*

- 4 terra-cotta statuettes including *At Guingamp, Brittany*; *Crouching Cat*; *Mare and Foal*; and *A Pig of Brittany*

- 1 plaster statuette titled *The Tennis Player*

- 2 wax models including the Afghan War Medal and *The Mistletoe*

- 1 wax model and plaster cast *The Girl I Left Behind Me*

- 1 wax model and colored cast titled *A Hunting Scene*

Exhibitions

1869 at the Royal Manchester Institution; included the hunting frieze of white paint on brown paper *At the Wrong End of the Wood*

1872 at the Dudley Gallery; included four sepia ink drawings called *Park Studies* and oil painting *At the Coverside*

1872 at the Royal Manchester Institution; included *Hunting Sketches*

1875 at the Dudley Gallery; included the sepia ink drawings *Breton Peasants, Doomed Lamb,* and *Mare and Foal*

1876 at the Royal Academy; included the oil painting *There were Three Ravens Sat on a Tree* and bas-relief *Horse Fair in Brittany*

1878 at the Grosvenor Gallery; included the bronze bas-relief *The Boar Hunt*

1878 at the Royal Academy; included the oil painting *The Three Huntsmen*

1881 at the Fine Art Society; included 300 original drawings

1881 at the Paris Salon; exhibition dedicated to the works of Caldecott, Walter Crane, and Kate Greenaway

1882 at the Royal Academy; included metal bas-relief *Scene from Spencer's 'Astrophel'*

1883 at a charity exhibition in Chester, Cheshire;

Caldecott donated several drawing and *Frogs*, a painting

1883 at the Institute of Painters in Water Colour; included watercolor painting *Putting the Hounds into Cover* reproduced in *Academy Sketches*

1884 at the Royal Manchester Institution; included the oil painting *May Day*

1885 at Hampstead, London; Caldecott donated about 15 original drawings

1885 at the Institute of Painters in Water Colour; included watercolor painting *The First Flight* reproduced in *Academy Sketches*

1886 at the Royal Manchester Institution; included the oil painting *The Girl I Left Behind Me*

1887 at the Manchester Jubilee Exhibition; included the bas-relief *The Three Jolly Huntsmen* and oil paintings *The Girl I Left Behind Me, May Day, Meeting of Shareholders Declaration of Dividend, and The Gardener's Little Daughter*

1888 at the Brasenose Club in Manchester; the memorial exhibition contained 173 of Caldecott's drawings, paintings, and sculptures

1890 at the Grosvenor Gallery; included the watercolor paintings *The Last Flight* and *Hunting*

1906 at the Royal Academy; included two drawings, both titled *Hunting Scene*

The Caldecott Medal Books

The following were published the year preceding the award year.

1938

Animals of the Bible, illustrated by Dorothy P. Lathrop, text selected by Helen Dean Fish (Lippincott)
Honor Books:
Seven Simeons: A Russian Tale, illustrated and retold by Boris Artzybasheff (Viking)
Four and Twenty Blackbirds . . ., illustrated by Robert Lawson, compiled by Helen Dean Fish (Stokes)

1939

Mei Li, illustrated and written by Thomas Handforth (Doubleday)
Honor Books:
The Forest Pool, illustrated and written by Laura Adams Armer (Longmans)
Wee Gillis, illustrated by Robert Lawson, written by Munro Leaf (Viking)
Snow White and the Seven Dwarfs, illustrated and translated by Wanda Gág (Coward-McCann)
Barkis, illustrated and written by Clare Turlay Newberry (Harper)

Andy and the Lion, illustrated and written by James Daugherty (Viking)

1940

Abraham Lincoln, illustrated and written by Ingri and Edgar Parin d'Aulaire (Doubleday)

Honor Books:

Cock-a Doodle Doo . . ., illustrated and written by Berta and Elmer Hader (Macmillan)

Madeline, illustrated and written by Ludwig Bemelmans (Viking)

The Ageless Story, illustrated by Lauren Ford, text from the Bible (Dodd Mead)

1941

They Were Strong and Good, illustrated and written by Robert Lawson (Viking)

Honor Book:

April's Kittens, illustrated and written by Clare Turlay Newberry (Harper)

1942

Make Way for Ducklings, illustrated and written by Robert McCloskey (Viking)

Honor Books:

An American ABC, illustrated and written by Maud and Miska Petersham (Macmillan)

In My Mother's House, illustrated by Velino Herrera, written by Ann Nolan Clark (Viking)

Paddle-to-the-Sea, illustrated and written by Holling C. Holling (Houghton Mifflin)

Nothing at All, illustrated and written by Wanda Gág (Coward-McCann)

1943

The Little House, illustrated and written by Virginia Lee Burton (Houghton Mifflin)

Honor Books:

Dash and Dart, illustrated and written by Mary and Conrad Buff (Viking)

Marshmallow, illustrated and written by Clare Turlay Newberry (Harper)

1944

Many Moons, illustrated by Louis Slobodkin, written by James Thurber (Harcourt)

Honor Books:

Small Rain: Verses from the Bible, illustrated by Elizabeth Orton Jones, verses selected by Jessie Orton Jones (Viking)

Pierre Pidgeon, illustrated by Arnold E. Bare, written by Lee Kingman (Houghton Mifflin)

The Mighty Hunter, illustrated and written by Berta and Elmer Hader (Macmillan)

A Child's Good Night Book, illustrated by Jean Charlot, written by Margaret Wise Brown (W. R. Scott)

The Good-Luck Horse, illustrated by Plato Chan, written by Chih-Yi Chan (Whittlesey)

1945

Prayer for a Child, illustrated by Elizabeth Orton Jones, written by Rachel Field (Macmillan)

Honor Books:

Mother Goose, illustrated by Tasha Tudor (Walck)

In the Forest, illustrated and written by Marie Hall Ets (Viking)

Yonie Wondernose, illustrated and written by Marguerite de Angeli (Doubleday)

The Christmas Anna Angel, illustrated by Kate Seredy, written by Ruth Sawyer (Viking)

1946

The Rooster Crows . . ., illustrated and text selected by Maud and Miska Petersham (Macmillan)

Honor Books:

Little Lost Lamb, illustrated by Leonard Weisgard, written by Golden MacDonald [pseudonym of Margaret Wise Brown] (Doubleday)

Sing Mother Goose, illustrated by Marjorie Torrey, music by Opal Wheeler (Dutton)

My Mother Is the Most Beautiful Woman in the World, illustrated by Ruth Gannett, retold by Becky Reyher (Lothrop)

You Can Write Chinese, illustrated and written by Kurt Wiese (Viking)

1947

The Little Island, illustrated by Leonard Weisgard, written by Golden MacDonald [pseudonym of Margaret Wise Brown] (Doubleday)

Honor Books:

Rain Drop Splash, illustrated by Leonard Weisgard, written by Alvin Tresselt (Lothrop)

The Boats on the River, illustrated by Jay Hyde Barnum, written by Marjorie Flack (Viking)

Timothy Turtle, illustrated by Tony Palazzo, written by Al Graham (Robert Welsh)

Pedro, the Angel of Olvera Street, illustrated and written by Leo Politi (Scribner)

Sing in Praise: A Collection of the Best-Loved Hymns, illustrated by Marjorie Torrey, stories of hymns and music arranged by Opal Wheeler (Dutton)

1948

White Snow, Bright Snow, illustrated by Roger Duvoisin, written by Alvin Tresselt (Lothrop)

Honor Books:

Stone Soup, illustrated and written by Marcia Brown (Scribner)

McElligot's Pool, illustrated and written by Dr. Seuss [pseudonym of Theodor Seuss Geisel] (Random House)

Bambino the Clown, illustrated and written by George Schreiber (Viking)

Roger and the Fox, illustrated by Hildegard Woodward, written by Lavinia R. Davis (Doubleday)

Song of Robin Hood, designed and illustrated by Virginia Lee Burton, text selected and edited by Anne Malcolmson (Houghton Mifflin)

1949

The Big Snow, illustrated and written by Berta and Elmer Hader (Macmillan)

Honor Books:

Blueberries for Sal, illustrated and written by Robert McCloskey (Viking)

All Around the Town, illustrated by Helen Stone, written by Phyllis McGinley (Lippincott)

Juanita, illustrated and written by Leo Politi (Scribner)

Fish in the Air, illustrated and written by Kurt Wiese (Viking)

1950

Song of the Swallows, illustrated and written by Leo Politi (Scribner)

Honor Books:

America's Ethan Allen, illustrated by Lynd Ward, written by Stewart Holbrook (Houghton Mifflin)

The Wild Birthday Cake, illustrated by Hildegarde Woodward, written by Lavinia R. Davis (Doubleday)

The Happy Day, illustrated by Marc Simont, written by Ruth Krauss (Harper)

Bartholomew and the Oobleck, illustrated and written by Dr. Seuss [pseudonym of Theodor Seuss Geisel] (Random House)

Henry-Fisherman, illustrated and written by Marcia Brown (Scribner)

1951

The Egg Tree, illustrated and written by Katherine Milhous (Scribner)

Honor Books:

Dick Whittington and His Cat, illustrated and written by Marcia Brown (Scribner)

The Two Reds, illustrated by Nicolas [pseudonym of

Nicolas Mordvinoff], written by Will [pseudonym of William Lipkind] (Harcourt)

If I Ran the Zoo, illustrated and written by Dr. Seuss [pseudonym of Theodor Seuss Geisel] (Random House)

The Most Wonderful Doll in the World, illustrated by Helen Stone, written by Phyllis McGinley (Lippincott)

T-Bone, the Baby-Sitter, illustrated and written by Clare Turlay Newberry (Harper)

1952

Finders Keepers, illustrated by Nicholas [pseudonym of Nicolas Mordvinoff], written by Will [pseudonym of William Lipkind] (Harcourt)

Honor Books:

Mr. T. W. Anthony Woo, illustrated and written by Marie Hall Ets (Viking)

Skipper John's Cook, illustrated and written by Marcia Brown (Scribner)

All Falling Down, illustrated by Margaret Bloy Graham, written by Gene Zion (Harper)

Bear Party, illustrated and written by William Pène du Bois (Viking)

Feather Mountain, illustrated and written by Elizabeth Olds (Houghton Mifflin)

1953

The Biggest Bear, illustrated and written by Lynd Ward (Houghton Mifflin)

Randolph Caldecott

Honor Books:

Puss in Boots, illustrated and translated by Marcia Brown (Scribner)

One Morning in Maine, illustrated and written by Robert McCloskey (Viking)

Ape in a Cape: An Alphabet of Odd Animals, illustrated and written by Fritz Eichenberg (Harcourt)

The Storm Book, illustrated by Margaret Bloy Graham, written by Charlotte Zolotow (Harper)

Five Little Monkeys, illustrated and written by Juliet Kepes (Houghton Mifflin)

1954

Madeline's Rescue, illustrated and written by Ludwig Bemelmans (Viking)

Honor Books:

Journey Cake, Ho!, illustrated by Robert McCloskey, written by Ruth Sawyer (Viking)

When Will the World Be Mine?, illustrated by Jean Charlot, written by Miriam Schlein (W. R. Scott)

The Steadfast Tin Soldier, illustrated by Marcia Brown, translated by M. R. James (Scribner)

A Very Special House, illustrated by Maurice Sendak, written by Ruth Krauss (Harper)

Green Eyes, illustrated and written by A. Birnbaum (Capitol)

1955

Cinderella, or the Little Glass Slipper, illustrated and translated from Charles Perrault by Marcia Brown (Scribner)

Honor Books:

Book of Nursery and Mother Goose Rhymes, illustrated and text selected by Marguerite de Angeli (Doubleday)

Wheel on the Chimney, illustrated by Tibor Gergely, written by Margaret Wise Brown (Lippincott)

The Thanksgiving Story, illustrated by Helen Sewell, written by Alice Dalgliesh (Scribner)

1956

Frog Went A-Courtin', illustrated by Feodor Rojankovsky, story retold by John Langstaff (Harcourt)

Honor Books:

Play With Me, illustrated and written by Marie Hall Ets (Viking)

Crow Boy, illustrated and written by Taro Yashima (Viking)

1957

A Tree Is Nice, illustrated by Marc Simont, written by Janice May Udry (Harper)

Honor Books:

Mr. Penny's Race Horse, illustrated and written by Marie Hall Ets (Viking)

1 Is One, illustrated and written by Tasha Tudor (Walck)

Anatole, illustrated by Paul Galdone, written by Eve Titus (McGraw-Hill)

Gillespie and the Guards, illustrated by James Daugherty, written by Benjamin Elkin (Viking)

Lion, illustrated and written by William Pène du Bois (Viking)

1958

Time of Wonder, illustrated and written by Robert McCloskey (Viking)

Honor Books:

Fly High, Fly Low, illustrated and written by Don Freeman (Viking)

Anatole and the Cat, illustrated by Paul Galdone, written by Eve Titus (McGraw-Hill)

1959

Chanticleer and the Fox, illustrated and adapted from Chaucer's *Canterbury Tales* by Barbara Cooney (Crowell)

Honor Books:

The House that Jack Built: La Maison Que Jacques A Batie, illustrated and written by Antonio Frasconi (Harcourt)

What Do You Say, Dear?, illustrated by Maurice Sendak, written by Sesyle Joslin (W. R. Scott)

Umbrella, illustrated and written by Taro Yashima (Viking)

1960

Nine Days to Christmas, illustrated by Marie Hall Ets, written by Marie Hall Ets and Aurora Labastida (Viking)

Honor Books:

Houses from the Sea, illustrated by Adrienne Adams, written by Alice E. Goudey (Scribner)

The Moon Jumpers, illustrated by Maurice Sendak, written by Janice May Udry (Harper)

1961

Baboushka and the Three Kings, illustrated by Nicholas Sidjakov, written by Ruth Robbins (Parnassus Press)

Honor Book:

Inch by Inch, illustrated and written by Leo Lionni (Ivan Obolensky)

1962

Once a Mouse, illustrated and retold by Marcia Brown (Scribner)

Honor Books:

The Fox Went Out on a Chilly Night: An Old Song, illustrated by Peter Spier (Doubleday)

Little Bear's Visit, illustrated by Maurice Sendak, written by Else Holmelund Minarik (Harper)

The Day We Saw the Sun Come Up, illustrated by Adrienne Adams, written by Alice E. Goudey (Scribner)

1963

The Snowy Day, illustrated and written by Ezra Jack Keats (Viking)

Honor Books:

The Sun Is a Golden Earring, illustrated by Bernarda Bryson, written by Natalia M. Belting (Holt)

Mr. Rabbit and the Lovely Present, illustrated by Maurice Sendak, written by Charlotte Zolotow (Harper)

1964

Where the Wild Things Are, illustrated and written by Maurice Sendak (Harper)

Honor Books:

Swimmy, illustrated and written by Leo Lionni (Pantheon)

All in the Morning Early, illustrated by Evaline Ness, written by Sorche Nic Leodhas [pseudonym of Leclaire Alger] (Holt)

Mother Goose and Nursery Rhymes, illustrated and text selected by Philip Reed (Atheneum)

1965

May I Bring a Friend?, illustrated by Beni Montresor, written by Beatrice Schenk de Regniers (Atheneum)

Honor Books:

Rain Makes Applesauce, illustrated by Marvin Bileck, written by Julian Scheer (Holiday House)

The Wave, illustrated by Blair Lent, written by Margaret Hodges (Houghton Mifflin)

A Pocketful of Cricket, illustrated by Evaline Ness, written by Rebecca Caudill (Holt)

1966

Always Room for One More, illustrated by Nonny Hogrogian, adapted by Sorche Nic Leodhas [pseudonym of Leclaire Alger] (Holt)

Honor Books:

Hide and Seek Fog, illustrated by Roger Duvoisin, written by Alvin Tresselt (Lothrop)

Just Me, illustrated by Marie Hall Ets (Viking)

Tom Tit Tot, illustrated by Evaline Ness, written by Joseph Jacobs (Scribner)

1967

Sam, Bangs and Moonshine, illustrated and written by Eveline Ness (Holt)

Honor Book:

One Wide River to Cross, illustrated by Ed Emberley, written by Barbara Emberley (Prentice-Hall)

1968

Drummer Hoff, illustrated by Ed Emberley, adapted by Barbara Emberley (Prentice-Hall)

Honor Books:

Seashore Story, illustrated and written by Taro Yashima (Viking)

Frederick, illustrated and written by Leo Lionni (Pantheon)

The Emperor and the Kite, illustrated by Ed Young, written by Jane Yolen (World)

1969

The Fool of the World and the Flying Ship, illustrated by Uri Shulevitz, retold by Arthur Ransome (Farrar)

Honor Book:

Why the Sun and the Moon Live in the Sky: An African Folktale, illustrated by Blair Lent, written by Elphinstone Dayrell (Houghton Mifflin)

1970

Sylvester and the Magic Pebble, illustrated and written by William Steig (Windmill Books)

Honor Books:

Alexander and the Wind-up Mouse, illustrated and written by Leo Lionni (Pantheon)

Goggles!, illustrated and written by Ezra Jack Keats (Macmillan)

Pop Corn & Ma Goodness, illustrated by Robert Andrew Parker, written by Edna Mitchell Preston (Viking)

The Judge: An Untrue Tale, illustrated by Margot Zemach, written by Harve Zemach (Farrar, Straus)

Thy Friend, Obadiah, illustrated and written by Brinton Turkle (Viking)

1971

A Story, A Story, illustrated and retold by Gail E. Haley (Atheneum)

Honor Books:

The Angry Moon, illustrated by Blair Lent, retold by William Sleator (Atlantic Little)

Frog and Toad Are Friends, illustrated and written by Arnold Lobel (Harper)

In the Night Kitchen, illustrated and written by Maurice Sendak (Harper)

1972

One Fine Day, illustrated and adapted by Nonny Hogrogian (Macmillan)

Honor Books:

Hildilid's Night, illustrated by Arnold Lobel, written by Cheli Durán Ryan (Macmillan)

If All the Seas Were One Sea, illustrated and written by Janina Domanska (Macmillan)

Moja Means One: Swahili Counting Book, illustrated by Tom Feelings, written by Muriel Feelings (Dial)

1973

The Funny Little Woman, illustrated by Blair Lent, retold
by Arlene Mosel (Dutton)

Honor Books:

Hosie's Alphabet, illustrated by Leonard Baskin, written
by Hosea, Tobias, and Lisa Baskin (Viking)

Snow-White and the Seven Dwarfs, illustrated by Nancy
Ekholm Burkert, translated by Randall Jarrell
(Farrar, Straus)

When Clay Sings, illustrated by Tom Bahti, written by
Byrd Baylor (Scribner)

Anansi the Spider, illustrated and written by Gerald
McDermott (Holt)

1974

Duffy and the Devil, illustrated by Margot Zemach, retold by Harve Zemach (Farrar)

Honor Books:

Cathedral: The Story of Its Construction, illustrated and
written by David Macaulay (Houghton Mifflin)

The Three Jovial Huntsmen, illustrated and written by
Susan Jeffers (Bradbury)

1975

Arrow to the Sun, illustrated and retold by Gerald
McDermott (Viking)

Honor Book:

Jambo Means Hello: A Swahili Alphabet Book, illustrated by Tom Feelings, written by Muriel Feelings
(Dial)

1976

Why Mosquitoes Buzz in People's Ears, illustrated by Leo and Diane Dillon, retold by Verna Aardema (Dial)

Honor Books:

Strega Nona, illustrated and retold by Tomie de Paola (Prentice-Hall)

The Desert Is Theirs, illustrated by Peter Parnall, written by Byrd Baylor (Scribner)

1977

Ashanti to Zulu: African Traditions, illustrated by Leo and Diane Dillon, written by Margaret Musgrove (Dial)

Honor Books:

The Amazing Bone, illustrated and written by William Steig (Farrar)

The Contest, illustrated and adapted by Nonny Hogrogian (Greenwillow)

Fish for Supper, illustrated and written by M. B. Goffstein (Dial)

The Golem: A Jewish Legend, illustrated and retold by Beverly Brodsky McDermott (Lippincott)

Hawk, I'm Your Brother, illustrated by Peter Parnall, written by Byrd Baylor (Scribner)

1978

Noah's Ark, illustrated and translated by Peter Spier (Doubleday)

Honor Books:

Castle, illustrated and written by David Macaulay (Houghton)

It Could Always Be Worse, illustrated and retold by Margot Zemach (Farrar)

1979
The Girl Who Loved Wild Horses, illustrated and written by Paul Goble (Bradbury)
Honor Books:
Freight Train, illustrated and written by Donald Crews (Greenwillow)
The Way to Start a Day, illustrated by Peter Parnall, written by Byrd Baylor (Scribner)

1980
Ox-Cart Man, illustrated by Barbara Cooney, written by Donald Hall (Viking)
Honor Books:
Ben's Trumpet, illustrated and written by Rachel Isadora (Greenwillow)
The Garden of Abdul Gasazi, illustrated and written by Chris Van Allsburg (Houghton)
The Treasure, illustrated and retold by Uri Shulevitz (Farrar)

1981
Fables, illustrated and written by Arnold Lobel (Harper)
Honor Books:
The Grey Lady and the Strawberry Snatcher, illustrated by Molly Bang (Four Winds)
The Bremen-Town Musicians, illustrated and retold by Ilse Plume (Doubleday)
Mice Twice, illustrated and written by Joseph Low

(Atheneum/McElderry)

Truck, illustrated and written by Donald Crews (Greenwillow)

1982

Jumanji, illustrated and written by Chris Van Allsburg (Houghton Mifflin)

Honor Books:

On Market Street, illustrated by Anita Lobel, written by Arnold Lobel (Greenwillow)

Outside Over There, illustrated and written by Maurice Sendak (Harper)

A Visit to William Blake's Inn: Poems for Innocent and Experienced Travelers, illustrated by Alice and Martin Provensen, written by Nancy Willard (Harcourt)

Where the Buffaloes Begin, illustrated by Stephen Gammell, written by Olaf Baker (Warne)

1983

Shadow, illustrated and translated by Marcia Brown (Scribner)

Honor Books:

A Chair for My Mother, illustrated and written by Vera B. Williams (Greenwillow)

When I Was Young in the Mountains, illustrated by Diane Goode, written by Cynthia Rylant (Dutton)

1984

The Glorious Flight: Across the Channel With Louis Blériot July 25, 1919, illustrated and written by Alice and Martin Provensen (Viking)

Honor Books:

Little Red Riding Hood, illustrated and retold by Trina Schart Hyman (Holiday)

Ten, Nine, Eight, illustrated and written by Molly Bang (Greenwillow)

1985

Saint George and the Dragon, illustrated by Trina Schart Hyman, retold by Margaret Hodges (Little Brown)

Honor Books:

Hansel and Gretel, illustrated by Paul O. Zelinsky, retold by Rika Lesser (Dodd)

Have You Seen My Duckling?, illustrated and written by Nancy Tafuri (Greenwillow)

The Story of Jumping Mouse, illustrated and written by John Steptoe (Lothrop)

1986

The Polar Express, illustrated and written by Chris Van Allsburg (Houghton Mifflin)

Honor Books:

King Bidgood's in the Bathtub, illustrated by Don Wood, written by Audrey Wood (Harcourt)

The Relatives Came, illustrated by Stephen Gammell, written by Cynthia Rylant (Bradbury)

1987

Hey, Al!, illustrated by Richard Egielski, written by Arthur Yorinks (Farrar)

Honor Books:

Rumplestiltskin, illustrated and written by Paul O. Zelinsky (Dodd)

The Village of Round and Square Houses, illustrated and written by Ann Grifalconi (Little, Brown)

Alphabatics, illustrated by Suse MacDonald (Bradbury)

1988

Owl Moon, illustrated by John Schoenherr, written by Jane Yolen (Philomel Books)

Honor Book:

Mufaro's Beautiful Daughters, illustrated and written by John Steptoe (Lothrop)

1989

Song and Dance Man, illustrated by Stephen Gammell, written by Karen Ackerman (Knopf)

Honor Books:

Mirandy and Brother Wind, illustrated by Jerry Pinkney, written by Patricia C. McKissack (Knopf)

Free Fall, illustrated and conceived by David Wiesner (Lothrop)

The Boy of the Three-Year Nap, illustrated by Allen Say, retold by Dianne Snyder (Houghton Mifflin)

Goldilocks and the Three Bears, illustrated and retold by James Marshall (Dial)

1990

Lon Po Po: A Red-Riding Hood Story from China, illustrated and translated by Ed Young (Philomel)

Honor Books:

Bill Peet: An Autobiography, illustrated and written by Bill Peet (Houghton Mifflin)

The Talking Eggs, illustrated by Jerry Pinkney, written by Robert D. San Souci (Dial)

Hershel and the Hanukkah Goblins, illustrated by Trina Schart Hyman, written by Eric Kimmel (Holiday House)

Color Zoo, illustrated and written by Lois Ehlert (Lippincott)

1991

Black and White, illustrated and written by David Macaulay (Houghton Mifflin)

Honor Books:

Puss in Boots, illustrated by Fred Marcellino, translated by Malcolm Arthur (Farrar)

"More More More," Said the Baby, illustrated and written by Vera B. Williams (Greenwillow)

1992

Tuesday, illustrated and written by David Wiesner (Clarion)

Honor Book:

Tar Beach, illustrated and written by Faith Ringgold (Crown)

1993 - *Mirette on the High Wire*, illustrated and written by Emily Arnold McCully (Putnam)

Honor Books:

Seven Blind Mice, illustrated and retold by Ed Young (Philomel)

The Stinky Cheese Man and Other Fairly Stupid Tales,

illustrated by Lane Smith, written by Jon Scieszka (Viking)

Working Cotton, illustrated by Carole Byard, written by Sherley Ann Williams (Harcourt)

1994

Grandfather's Journey, illustrated and written by Allen Say (Houghton Mifflin)

Honor Books:

In the Small, Small Pond, illustrated and written by Denise Fleming (Holt)

Owen, illustrated and written by Kevin Henkes (Greenwillow)

Peppe the Lamplighter, illustrated by Ted Lewin, written by Elisa Bartone (Lothrop)

Raven: A Trickster Tale from the Pacific Northwest, illustrated and retold by Gerald McDermott (Harcourt)

Yo! Yes?, illustrated and written by Chris Raschka (Orchard)

1995

Smoky Night, illustrated by David Diaz, written by Eve Bunting (Harcourt Brace)

Honor Books:

Swamp Angel, illustrated by Paul O. Zelinsky, written by Anne Isaacs (Dutton)

John Henry, illustrated by Jerry Pinkney, written by Julius Lester (Dial)

Time Flies, illustrated and conceived by Eric Rohmann (Crown)

1996

Officer Buckle and Gloria, illustrated and written by
Peggy Rathmann (Putnam)

Honor Books:

Alphabet City, illustrated and conceived by Stephen P.
Johnson (Viking)

Zin! Zin! Zin! a Violin, illustrated by Marjorie Priceman,
written by Lloyd Moss (Simon and Schuster)

The Faithful Friend, illustrated by Brian Pinkney, retold
by Robert D. San Souci (Simon and Schuster)

Tops and Bottoms, illustrated and retold by Janet Stevens
(Harcourt)

1997

Golem, illustrated and retold by David Wisniewski
(Clarion)

Honor Books:

Hush!: A Thai Lullaby, illustrated by Holly Meade, written by Minfong Ho (Orchard)

The Graphic Alphabet, illustrated and conceived by
David Pelletier (Orchard)

The Paperboy, illustrated and written by Dav Pilkey
(Orchard)

Starry Messenger: Galileo Galilei, illustrated and written by Peter Sis (Farrar)

1998

Rapunzel, illustrated and retold by Paul O. Zelinsky
(Dutton)

Honor Books:

Harlem, illustrated by Christopher Myers, written by

Walter Dean Myers (Scholastic)

The Gardener, illustrated by David Small, written by Sara Stewart (Farrar)

There Was an Old Lady Who Swallowed a Fly, illustrated and retold by Simms Taback (Viking)

1999

Snowflake Bentley, illustrated by Mary Azarian, written by Jacqueline Briggs Martin (Houghton Mifflin)

Honor Books:

Duke Ellington, illustrated by Brian Pinkney, written by Andrea Davis Pinkney (Hyperion)

No, David!, illustrated and written by David Shannon (Scholastic)

Snow, illustrated and written by Uri Shulevitz (Farrar)

Tibet: Through the Red Box, illustrated and written by Peter Sis (Farrar)

2000

Joseph Had a Little Overcoat, illustrated and written by Simms Taback (Viking)

Honor Books:

A Child's Calendar, illustrated by Trina Schart Hyman, written by John Updike (Holiday House)

Sector 7, illustrated and written by David Weisner (Clarion)

When Sophie Gets Angry—Really, Really Angry, illustrated and written by Molly Bang (Scholastic)

The Ugly Duckling, illustrated and adapted by Jerry Pinkney, written by Hans Christian Andersen (Morrow)

2001

So You Want to Be President?, illustrated by David Small, written by Judith St. George (Philomel)

Honor Books:

Casey at the Bat, illustrated by Christopher Bing, written by Ernest Lawrence Thayer (Handprint)

Click, Clack, Moo: Cows That Type, illustrated by Betsy Lewin, written by Doreen Cronin (Simon & Schuster)

Olivia, illustrated and written by Ian Falconer (Atheneum)

2002

The Three Pigs, illustrated and written by David Wiesner (Clarion/Houghton Mifflin)

Honor Books:

The Dinosaurs of Waterhouse Hawkins, illustrated by Brian Selznick, written by Barbara Kerley (Scholastic)

Martin's Big Words: the Life of Dr. Martin Luther King, Jr., illustrated by Bryan Collier, written by Doreen Rappaport (Jump at the Sun/Hyperion)

The Stray Dog, illustrated and written by Marc Simont (HarperCollins)

2003

My Friend Rabbit, illustrated and written by Eric Rohmann (Roaring Brook Press/Millbrook Press)

Honor Books:

The Spider and the Fly, illustrated by Tony DiTerlizzi, based on a tale by Mary Howitt (Simon & Schuster)

Randolph Caldecott

Hondo & Fabian, illustrated and written by Peter
McCarty (Henry Holt)
Noah's Ark, illustrated and written by Jerry Pinkney (Sea
Star/North-South Books)

References

Alderson, Brian, *Sing a Song for Sixpence: The English Picture Book Tradition and Randolph Caldecott*, Cambridge and New York: Cambridge University Press, 1986.

Billington, Elizabeth T., *The Randolph Caldecott Treasury*, New York: Frederick Warne, 1978.

Blackburn, Henry, *Randolph Caldecott: A Personal Memoir of His Early Art Career*, London: Sampson Low, Marston Searle & Rivington, 1887.

Crane, Walter, *An Artist's Reminiscences*, London: The Macmillan Company, 1907.

Davis, Mary Gould, *Randolph Caldecott*, Philadelphia: Lippincott, 1946.

Egielski, Richard, "Caldecott Medal Acceptance," *The Horn Book Magazine*, July/August 1987, page 433.

Engen, Rodney K., *Randolph Caldecott: Lord of the Nursery*, London: Bloomsbury Books, 1976.

Hutchins, Michael, editor, *Yours Pictorially: Illustrated Letters of Randolph Caldecott*, London and New York: Frederick Warne, 1976.

Kingman, Lee, *Newbery and Caldecott Medal Books 1976-1985*, Boston: The Horn Book, Inc., 1986.

Lewis, Marguerite, *Randolph Caldecott: The Children's Illustrator*, Hagerstown, MD: Alleyside Press, 1992.

Marcus, Leonard S., "Medal Man: Randolph Caldecott

and the Art of the Picture Book," *Horn Book*, March/ April 2001, pp. 155-170.

Miller, Bertha Mahony and Elinor Whitney Field, *Caldecott Medal Books 1938-1957*, Boston: The Horn Book, Inc., 1957.

Overton, Jacqueline, "Randolph Caldecott" in *Contemporary Illustrators of Children's Books*, edited by Bertha E. Mahony and Elinor Whitney, Boston: Women's Educational and Industrial Union, 1930.

Sendak, Maurice, *Caldecott and Co.: Notes on Books and Pictures*, New York: Farrar, Straus and Giroux, 1988.

Smith, Irene, *A History of the Newbery and Caldecott Medals*, New York: Viking, 1957.

Spielman, M. H. and G. S. Layard, *Kate Greenaway*, London: Benjamin Blom, 1905.

Van Stockum, Hilda, "Caldecott's Pictures in Motion," *Horn Book Magazine*, Volume 22, 1946, pp.119-25.

Websites
   http://www.ala.org/alsc/caldecott.html
   http://www.caldecottfoundation.org
   http://www.randolphcaldecott.org.uk
   http://www.rscamerica.com   (Randolph   Caldecott
   Society of America)

Index

About the Author

CLAUDETTE HEGEL is a longtime fan and collector of everything Caldecott. She serves as regional advisor for the Minnesota Society of Children's Book Writers and Illustrators. Claudette Hegel lives in New Hope, Minnesota.

Photo by David Dyer-Bennet

J92 Caldecott
Hegel, Claudette
Randolph Caldecott :

$27.50   3/4/05   AHB-4576